TIME TO SPEAK

Yeshua and Yaakov:
The Journey of Two Brothers

By

Justin James

Dedication

To all beings: may you find your way beyond the feeling of separation, join with Divinity, and be Love.

First paperback edition December 2018

ISBN-13: 978-0-9600721-0-1

Kaja Publishing
Justin©justinjames01.com

Cover designs by Sam Elliott and Tavis Taylor
Original painting with Yeshua by Greg Olsen
© Greg Olsen. By arrangement with Greg Olsen Art, Inc.
For information on art prints by Greg Olsen please visit,
www.GregOlsen.com or call 1-800-352-0107.

Contents

TIME TO SPEAK

Forward

We initially referred to this work as "the James Project," this is, until Yaakov spoke. Identifying his name as Yaakov and not James was in itself a major detail for us and made a great impact. Further research explained that James is English for Jacob, which is the Latin form of the Hebrew Yaakov. We were immediately getting new information that directed us to new truths, which became the theme for this project: Truth.

So who was this James/Yaakov guy anyway? Why would I, or anyone, be interested in James/Yaakov? How did this project get started? How did it develop?

James, also known as "James the Just," was the brother of Jesus. Jesus is referred to in this book by the name Yaakov called him: Yeshua, which is the Hebrew pronunciation of Jeshua. James was head of Jewish Christianity, and was known historically as "the Bishop of Jerusalem" after the ascension of Yeshua. He was known for maintaining Jewish law while taking up "Christian" leadership after the ascension and was esteemed by the Jewish leadership until his death, somewhere between 62-69 AD.

"We are aware that you will depart from us. Who will be our leader?" Jesus said to them, "No matter where you come [from] it is to James the Just that you shall go, for whose sake heaven and earth have come to exist."
[*The Gospel of Thomas*, *The Nag Hammadi Scriptures*, by Marvin W. Meyer]

Clement of Rome (30-97 CE), or someone purporting to be him, addresses his letter in the non-canonical Pseudo-Clementine Homilies of Clement to "James... the Bishop of Bishops, who rules Jerusalem, the Holy Assembly of the Hebrews and the Assemblies everywhere," as does Peter similarly in his Homilies letter.

Jewish contemporary of James, knows about him, and even insists that James' death was the reason the Jewish people believed Jerusalem fell: "These things [the Uprising and consequent destruction of Jerusalem by the Romans] happened to the Jews in requital for James the Righteous, who was a brother of Jesus known as Christ, for though he was the most Righteous of men, [they] put him to death."
[http://www.thenazareneway.com/james_the_brother_of_jesus.htm]

This guy James/Yaakov sounds like an important fellow. How did he come to be in charge after Yeshua ascended? Where did he come from? We don't hear much about him in the four gospels of the New Testament. Mathew, Mark, Luke and John all take turns at relating what they think are important about Jesus' life and death. James isn't mentioned, except in passing, until after the ascension when Jesus tells the apostles that James is in charge. But you won't find that in your council of Nicaea-approved biblical text. That instruction is in the Gnostic text of Thomas. There is still little said in the Bible after that time about him, indeed there is more confusion as to which James it is, as there are so many men referred to by that name in the Bible. More seems recorded about James the Just in the secular historical record than the Bible per the references above.

Where did the title of this book come from? Archangel Gabriel said it is "Time to Speak" and recommended this as a title to Maggie, who guided me in my hypnosis regression to Yaakov. The Brothers wanted to include the remainder of the title to emphasize their relationship and journey, which is represented by the cover photo. For the rest, let us start from concepts.

What brought me to this point? The answer is complex. I read the book, "Anna, Grandmother of Jesus," recommended by my friends Barbara/Aaron, before embarking on a trip to southern England. I joined a trip with new friends on a lark. We would be walking sacred sites in Glastonbury, Cornwall and other sites in southern England that did not have much meaning to me, yet. Though I had no particular interest in going to England at the time, I felt compelled when the opportunity arose. Having learned to listen to these little nudges, though not usually understanding the import at the time, I always have more clarity later and in hindsight I am glad I paid attention. In this book when Anna talked about her grandchildren, I began to hear a voice calling me "James." James?? Me?? Are you referring to me as James in this book, brother of Jeshua? Spirit confirmed: "Yes." I have a great deal of wariness about clarity of message from spirit when it concerns myself, as I do not want to receive distortions based upon ego. So, I go to others I trust, one of whom is Aaron.

Aaron's last incarnation on Earth was as a 15th century monk. He presently is in spirit form and works with Barbara Brodsky, who channels him. The two of them have spent thirty years educating and enlightening all who will listen with books, workshops, small groups and private meetings. They are the founders of Deep Spring Center in Ann Arbor, MI, which brings forward messages of non-duality without dogma or religious denomination. You may access a wealth of written and video-taped information at their website www.deepspring.org. Aaron is a master teacher of Love and Compassion. He explains complex spiritual concepts for our contemporary culture and minds. He accesses the Akashic records and interacts with highly polarized positive beings who bring us necessary information to assist in our healing and enlightenment. I turn to him with questions of such deep importance as this.

I have to admit, when I first met Aaron, I was a bit skeptical. Healthy skepticism is wise. However, after working with Barbara and Aaron for several years, I have come to trust their process and messages implicitly. They are consistent, always present from a place of love and compassion, and as far as I can ascertain, accurate.

As we go forward, I will share my many skepticisms regarding our process and journey. For it is a journey that we invite you to share with us, on many levels. A journey that requires one to at least suspend disbelief, if one cannot believe at first. That is where I started, with skepticism and a requirement to suspend disbelief. A journey of trust; a journey back into time; a journey of thoughts, feelings, courage, sacrifice, dedication, adventure, love and compassion. A journey to knowledge lost and now regained.

It is to Aaron I then turned for this big question: *am I James, brother of Jeshua?* He paused for a moment, seeking an answer, "Yes, you were James, brother of Jeshua." If ever the phrase "Oh my God" was appropriate, now was certainly the time. I avidly completed reading Anna's book and then the sequel about the Magdalenes. Many people spoke. But there was no voice for James. If James was really Jeshua's brother and James helped with the resurrection, why isn't he discussed further? Why didn't he come through in the sequel? I was told, "Because you are him and it is time for your voice to be heard, but it can only be heard through you. It is time to tell your story."

Oh, great. How am I supposed to tell this story? The Anna's author used hypnosis for channeling. I can channel but would never trust myself with this information. I had a fear that my mundane mind would distort the information, that my past reading might corrupt messages. I had never been hypnotized, desiring way too much control over my conscious mind to allow that. I did not know anyone who was a professional hypnotist; county fair entertainers didn't count. I considered writing an email to the author of "the Voice of the Magdalenes." She would probably think I was a kook. What to do next?

So, I went on my trip to England, armed with a totally new perspective about the lands and people and culture we were visiting. I saw landscapes I would recognize in my journey later as Yaakov. But I am getting ahead of myself.

Upon further discussion it was clear that a past life regression hypnosis session would be the best method to use for this project. And a dear friend, after much persuasion, agreed to facilitate the hypnosis sessions; we will call her "Maggie" as one of the Magdalenes.

The importance and impact of this project was such that it needed to be conducted in the most sacred and professional manner possible. I knew this person could accomplish this. And she did, in a most excellent and uncompromising way. I needed to have trust in her on many levels: for the integrity of the material; the integrity of self; the safety of myself under hypnosis; and to trust her with the knowledge of who I am. This was major stuff. If it was not for this facilitator, I could not have trusted her or the process as sincerely and the outcome may not have been as profound and exciting as it has become.

There were several months of anticipatory discreet preparations. I was not sure how these sessions would go and did not want to talk about them until afterwards, if at all. We cleared our calendars, set up space, and then struggled with technology. My voice does not project well, so we had recording issues. The first two sessions on the first day did not record at an audible level. We had to find different solutions and were finally able to set up a system that could capture both (all) our voices.

Maggie recommended a test run first: go under hypnosis to test and see if I could be hypnotized and hear what might come up. She explained the process she would use and we agreed on cues and safety issues. Lights out via a mask, recorder, action: I asked to be taken back to a life I knew when I had been a Druid. I knew no details other than I had been a Druid warrior priest and was helping to safeguard our ways from destruction by the Romans. I was completely unprepared for what was revealed during that session, and a personal message therein confirmed my access to that hypnotic regressed state.

While under hypnosis. I was fully cognizant of what I was seeing, hearing, saying, and experiencing. I expected that I would "go to sleep" and awaken with recorded information to then listen to. I was wrong. Maggie explained afterwards that the hypnotic state is similar to a deep meditation state where we are still conscious. It was like stepping into a movie and being a part of it. This is different from being told an event, such as when Aaron reveals information. That way, I only know what he is telling me. I can make up in my mind's eye images he may describe, but other details won't be there, and I cannot glean anything more than what he relates to me verbally; and I usually do not recall all of that accurately. Under hypnosis, inside the movie, I look around and can see and hear, experience details and nuances. And, I can now later step back into that scene and bring up images. These images are now a part of my memory experiences, unlike verbal descriptions I would have gotten by merely listening to myself talk. It has been a fascinating experience.

Experiencing past life regression and recollecting memories was very exciting. The informational content was fascinating. Many unforeseen and amazing experiences occurred during this process. Time and time again our process was legitimately confirmed by information or nuances revealed that neither of us knew about. We could hear the age progression of Yaakov as he talked to us as a child, then teen, then young adult and then older adult. We had no idea what information was coming from moment to moment, but it all ebbed and flowed and had presence and importance. The Burmese quote was a total surprise. I don't speak other languages, certainly not Burmese, and didn't know this to be a specific language (so now you know my ignorance about languages). We had other guest speakers come in to speak whom you will meet, again, totally unexpected.

Yeshua agreed to review the transcripts while incorporated in Barbara to provide unbiased comment. His comment after review of the first Yaakov summary discussing a day in young Yaakov's life reveals his humor and love, and a resonance of truth. The second and third transcripts are about early teen and adult times.

The last transcript has the information most people are interested in: the crux of Yeshua's reason for being here. Unexpectedly, upon review of this section, our spirit helpers were so excited about this project, they added important information to expand our knowledge they now determined we were ready for. I won't ruin the surprise of who comes in to speak, but I find it very exciting and am honored they shared this project with us.

The transcripts were written verbatim, in regular type, with only occasional grammar corrections. You will see/hear as the speaker pauses, contemplates, searches for words in efforts to describe what is occurring or what is necessary to pass on to you. We hope you can sense the conversational tone and sincerity as you read.

I sometimes added clarity I saw or garnered while in that space and this is added in *italics* with some redundancy, but I did not want to replace any of Yaakov's transcripts with my words, as I wanted to maintain integrity of his.

Personally, I don't like leaving a subject to go to a footnote or back to another area of a book for clarification despite its literary correctness to do so. I added clarifications and notes along the way to keep on topic and I hope you find it helpful.

Our reviewing guest speakers, to differentiate from our in-process guest speakers, were channeled by Barbara Brodsky, recordings transcribed by Janice Keller, and I copied these into appropriate places, so these are verbatim as well. A large section is added in its entirety after the Yaakov transcripts.

Maggie was crucial to hold sacred, safe space as I traveled back to be Yaakov, and as other guests channeled in. We have a complex process of hypnosis with past life regression: myself to Yaakov, and then Yaakov stepping aside for me to allow other guests to speak, with both myself and Yaakov able to still listen and remember these other guests' words. As I regressed to Yaakov, I had the distinct awareness of Yaakov thinking about every question asked as he was trying to give an accurate and complete answer. When others were speaking, I had no concept of thinking about what was being said, words simply flowed, I was not in charge of those words at all as either myself or Yaakov. On the recordings, the voices are all different. Those channeled are usually stronger, clearer, with a stream of consciousness that simply flows; as opposed to Yaakov's quiet, very deliberate, often searching speech.

Maggie was heartfelt and open to spirit herself. She asked pertinent questions to help draw out nuances and information that needed to be shared. She said afterwards she was often led by spirit about what to ask.

I do have to apologize for some formatting errors. Try as I might, I could not divide up some of the paragraphs that insisted on staying together, which resulted in some large bottom margins on a few pages.

This entire project has become an exciting and pertinent one for our present and past times as Earth dwellers and beings of spirit. We are so thankful and honored to have been led, coached, loved and supported during this entire process. What started out as a secret project for two wary people has manifested into a work of so many loving beings, incarnate and discarnate.

Welcome, we are excited for you to join us on this journey. As the title states,

It is time to speak.

Justin James

Disclaimer

There are references in this book from the Bible. This book and its message is not meant for only a Christian audience. In fact, some information will be controversial for many of a traditional Christian faith. This book is meant for anyone open to love and compassion. It is our hope everyone who reads this information will embark on a path of self-discovery and reconsideration of how they walk through this world.

For those not familiar with the Christian Bible, it is a compilation of written works approved by a group of Bishops in the 4th century, the council of Nicaea or the Nicene Council. Their intent was to provide a work of material they determined was most accurate. Any other material was considered "heretical," not approved. This process left out many works which are accurate. Throughout our world, there are works from many Masters that are accurate, yet not considered Christian or Christ-like and not included in the Christian Bible. Maybe we need to get rid of labels that separate us.

The Bible is composed of the Old Testament and the New Testament. The Old Testament is similar to the Torah. There are some differences between the Hebrew Torah and the Christian Old Testament, but much is similar. The New Testament attempts to chronicle Jesus and his message, predominately in the books of Mathew, Mark, Luke and John. It is to the events chronicled in these books which we have discussed herein. You may want to reference these books in the New Testament to help you understand the context of some of this book.

Reflections Upon Hypnosis Sessions with Facilitator
May 23-26, 2017

I have read many books, excerpts on early Christianity and read "Anna, Grandmother of Jesus" and the sequel "The Voice of the Magdalenes." I have concerns about bias and that is why I chose hypnosis instead of simply channeling James/Yaakov, brother of Yeshua. Hypnosis is not a state of deep subconscious, almost akin to unconscious, which I mistakenly thought it would be. Instead, it is more like a deep meditation where I can be aware of my present physical surroundings. I find myself frequently second-guessing myself. Am I making up what I am seeing from what I have read, or I am truly experiencing it? Some things are such that I would not have been able to make them up, so they are more easily acceptable. When I first realized I experienced an event or scene I could not make up, I relaxed more; but I still found myself second-guessing. Time is altered. What feels like 20-30 minutes is often one hour. Maggie stated she often waited quite a while for an answer although it only felt like a minute or so to me.

First session was Tuesday May 23, 2017. We did a practice session I will recall under the title "Friend," which follows.

Thursday, May 25, 2017. Barbara and I were visiting, and she inquired how the session went and was curious about whatever I would like to share. I first shared the story of the "Friend," for it was totally unexpected and would help lend credence to the process. Then I gave highlights of Yaakov's excerpts. That same morning, Barbara and I had been having discussions with Aaron, Yeshua, Fr. John, Fr. Kindness, and Dr. O, so I simply asked Yeshua if these memories were accurate and he responded, "Yes, but sometimes as a younger brother you were a pain in the neck!" in a loving and teasing way. He went on to say he would not say more but wait for our sessions over the next two days to be completed so as not to interfere with the process. Then we could meet and he would answer any further questions.

We recorded all sessions. The first recording is not reproducible, as I talked too softly for the internal microphone on the computer to pick it up. Subsequently, these sessions were typed from memory immediately after the sessions and are presented in summary form instead of verbatim transcript form. We used a headset with an external microphone for the remaining recordings and this worked well. Playback to me suggests Yaakov had a different voice and Maggie confirmed the voice was different from mine.

Maggie's questions were sometimes from a list I made and others from her intuition of the moment. She can feel when the energy changes, when certain beings present as Yeshua or as Grandmother. She can feel Yaakov's mood and energy as well. Thanks to her expertise and intuition, these discussions were quite fluid and creative in their flow.

Friend

Tuesday, May 23, 2017

This is the recollection of a practice hypnosis session for the "James Project" written that afternoon. Its message was a surprise and of profound meaning for me.

We start in a grove. This is the safe space I enter prior to transporting during hypnosis to another time. I see a moss-covered log by a pond with a spring at one end, the spring is a little higher than the pond so that it streams down into it. Tall deciduous trees are all around. It is a comfortable temperature, not hot, with a light breeze rustling through the greenery and over my skin. Yeshua is there to meet me. We hug like long-time friends that have not seen each other in a while: smiles, a hug, back slapping, standing back to look at each other with loving grins. With Maggie's prompting, I start to descend stairs, stairs that sometimes look like pavers and others like hard-packed dirt kept in place with logs. Yeshua appears at the bottom of the steps, waiting. Maggie prompts there is a transparent door with a swirling light on the other side. In my own time, I can step through and go where I need to.

As soon as I step through the light, I am standing and leaning forward, handing a leather-wrapped item, flat in my left hand, about the same size as my palm, to a man sitting just out of arm's reach so that he needs to lean forward to accept it. He is in his late 20s-30s, face indistinct, wearing a collection of wool and fur clothing. The sky is overcast, but not raining. His name is "Comrade," and I am being told it is my father in my present 21st century life. In the previous life being shown, he is my friend, comrade, someone I can always count on for support, assistance and love, regardless of the situation. I am being reminded this is who he is, even now in the present.

As I look around there is a fire in a firepit just to my right. Beyond that there are people sitting, talking or working, others milling about further beyond the fire circle, behind and to my right. Behind me is the village, simple wooden huts, furs and wooden furniture inside.

I live alone. Dedicating my life to studying and protecting. Studying with the elders, protecting them and our ways of being, ways of thinking. The Romans have been raiding other villages and destroying these things we hold dear and killing those of us who practice these ways. We hear they are merciless.

Comrade helps protect the village but is not as interested in the teachings. He respects the elders, as we all do; we depend upon their knowledge for healing and rituals of life and seasons of life.

Comrade is opening the gift. It is a large trapezoid-shaped grey stone, shorter at the top than the bottom, about 3 inches wide at the top, 4 inches wide at the bottom, about 4 inches long, 1/2-3/4 inches thick, flattened, with a red stone at the top embedded in it, like a large amulet.

The importance of this image is twofold:

-Denoting my father's steadfast friendship, even in times that are difficult or frustrating. Reminding me of how he would be if I were in the situation he is in presently.

-My role as Druid-warrior-priest.

This heartfelt image of my comrade-father is very profound. Even as I write this now, it stirs strong emotions of thankfulness and my own personal need to do a better job of being his friend in this life as he struggles with his health.

Day 1
Tuesday, May 23, 2017

Yaakov

This is the second session for the morning. I return to the grove from where I entered the first session, "Friend." It is a safe place to meet and start these journeys. Yeshua is there to meet me immediately and this time accompanied by an adult male a little shorter than he with shorter hair identified as James. The two brothers welcome me as a blessing to this journey. Yeshua and I greet and embrace like the first session. With Maggie's prompting, I start to descend the stairs. Yeshua appears at the bottom of the steps, waiting. James is behind, but I don't feel his presence as I descend the stairs.

I am already on a dirt road as a young boy, when Maggie instructs me to go through the transparent door with the white swirly light. I go back and go through the door and the light, and end up back on the same road. I apparently do not need the prompting to get to where I need to go anymore.

The scenery expands: there is another boy, a little older, playing, it's my brother, "Yeshua." There is a well about 20 ft to the right of me. As I look around, there are other boys about the same age and we are playing a game with a stick and a hoop, keeping it rolling on the ground. What I thought was the road, I see as I expand my view, is more of a central area of the village. I am seven. I am called "Yakov"(in Hebrew it is spelled Yaakov). As I look around I see stone houses beyond the well, adults walking around busy with duties. Some girls watching but not playing. This is a boys' game.

Scene shift

We are in a home, low ceiling, fireplace to the left. Long plank table in the center running ninety degrees from the fireplace. Far enough away from the fireplace for Grandmother to sit in front of the fireplace but not at the table. Mother is sitting on the other side of the table holding one of my sisters, gently rocking her as we listen to Grandmother. Yeshua is sitting to the left of Grandmother as I look at them, her right, on his knees on the dirt floor, but sitting back upright, intently listening. I am sitting next on one of the long benches of the table. The door is behind me to the left, it is open, and sunlight is coming in through here and a window on the wall across the table to the right of Mother. Father is there in the periphery of my vision as are two other siblings, but I am not paying much attention to them.

Grandmother is teaching, as she often does. She is teaching about "the Truth." The truth that we know, as we are taught and as we live as a family and village. The truth that Yeshua, the "chosen one," will one day teach to the world. When asked about learning and teaching, I see a stone building up a hill behind the village where the rabbi teaches. I must wait until I am twelve to enter here for lessons, but Grandmother has been teaching us already from a young age-girls and boys.

The Truth: our Creator is one of unconditional love. We are to love one another in like fashion. Without violence or jealousy, with sharing, teaching, learning and growing. Girls/women are just as important as boys/men. Grandmother has certainly always been a strong leader in our family. It is expected that women have a status of love and respect in my family.

I am being told the importance of these scenes is to show the importance of family life and we were a loving and supportive family. We all had roles for the future work Yeshua will be doing, it is the work of ALL of us, as a community, as a family. We live at Mt. Carmel.

Later, Yeshua is in temple, learning. He is answering questions posed by the rabbi and begins to expand on a topic that is beyond his learning. In subtle ways it differs from the rabbi's knowledge and understanding. The rabbi challenges him with another question, which he answers beyond what is expected. The rabbi appears surprised, annoyed, and then chastises Yeshua.

We have been taught from a young age to think and discern, and we have been given some teachings that are different from the local rabbinical teachings. Even though we live within a group of common religious thoughts and teachings, some of Grandmother's teachings are different.

Next scene

I am on the deck of a wooden ship sailing on open water. The sun is out, wind is steady. My uncle owns the ship. He and my grandmother are going to see my brother who has been gone for a year and I get to go with them. I am fourteen. I am anxious to see my brother who has been gone to a foreign land studying. I am anxious to hear what he has learned and see how he has grown. I am proud that I have grown and hope he is approving. I am enjoying this trip of sailing on the water.

Day 2
May 25, 2017

Travel and Training

Induction:
{Yeshua is in the grove, but also a small woman. Mother? No, Grandmother. I descend the stairs and wait for instructions to go through the door. This time I pause in the circular light tunnel and see that the lights are the stars, the cosmos rotating around, and I am in the middle as it swirls around me vertically. ~~ Justin}

Maggie tries to give a gift to me to take on the journey as recommended by spirit: a remote control to aid me to see (expand my vision or see details, limitless knowledge is available.)
I deferred the gift, said it's not needed and descended the steps to the portal. Once through the portal:

Yv: The ship has landed and there are a lot of people around. I am Yaakov.

M: Describe the scene.

Yv: It's a beach area with a path and cliffs, dirt and boulders, up on the hillside is shrubs and trees. It's a landing that has been used for many, many years.
We're going to walk up.

{We are landing in a bay that I recognize as Nanjizel, England. A bay that as early as 600BC has been used by tin merchants to obtain tin from these lands and take it back to our lands. We have disembarked from a voyage that was about three weeks. There is a flurry of activity as supplies are being organized and we are getting ready to walk up a steep dirt hill to the cliffs above as we proceed to the camps where Yeshua is staying. ~~ Justin}

M: Who's the "we?"

Yv: My uncle, my grandmother, and a lot of other people on the boat and some people who were on the shore to greet us. They are unloading items he has brought.

M: What are they unloading?

Yv: Items for our trip inland.

M: Supplies?

Yv: Yes.

M: How are you feeling?

Yv: Excited! Excited because I know I am going to see Yeshua, and the other camps. It's all a new experience. We're expecting to meet a lot of new people, a different way of life.

M: What have you been told about what to expect when you arrive?

Yv: There will be elders that I am to treat with respect like I do my grandmother. These are people Uncle and Grandmother have known for many, many years. They have lived among them in the past. Before we were born.

M: Are they like your people or different?

Yv: They are different. They have a different religion and a different way of life. It's much colder and damp up here.

M: Can you feel the coldness and dampness?

Yv: It's um...It's a cloudy, cloudy day. I feel the wind and hear the surf. There are seagulls above, or some type of bird.

M: Is this a very different land than where you came from?

Yv: Yes.

M: How old are you now, Yaakov?

Yv: Fourteen.

M: How long since you have seen your brother, Yeshua?

Yv: It's been a year. A year and a few months.

M: So, this is the first day you've arrived?

Yv: Yes, we've just arrived.

M: What will you do today?

Yv: They're going to unload the boat and carry it (the supplies) up the hill, and we're going to walk to the camp where my brother is. They say its two days' walk.

M: Who is telling you it's two days' walk?

Yv: General, um, it's repeated over and over by Uncle, Grandmother, and everybody around. They are excited and anxious. Just telling everyone "two days' walk."

M: So, everyone's excited, not just you?

Yv: Yes.

M: Seems like a very important day with a purpose. Can you tell us about the purpose of the trip in general?

Yv: Yeshua went for training amongst the people here, and ah, I wasn't allowed to go, it's only for him, and I was young.

M: Because of what when you were young?

Yv: The training was only for him, and I was younger. So, they only brought him, and he's been living with them all this time studying and training.

M: Does this group he is training and studying with have a name?

Yv: We know them as the Druids, but there's another name, but it's not quite clear...something about "the Masters," but there is more to it than that.

M: The Masters/Druids training, is there something you can tell us about the training or is there something secret about it?

Yv: Masters of the Wind, Masters of the Sea, Masters of the Woods...those are the names being shared.

M: Thank you. Will you be allowed to participate in the training now that you are older?

Yv: This is just a visit to check on Yeshua.

M: What would you like to tell us about the purpose of this visit?

Yv: It's just to check on him. See how his training is going. See if it is time for him to return with us. They don't think it will be.

M: Who will decide if it is time, if he's ready?

Yv: The Masters, my uncle and grandmother.

M: The Masters along with your grandmother?

Yv: Yes, the Masters, uncle and my grandmother, they will all make that decision.

M: Will you tell us a little about your uncle? What is your relationship like with him? What's his personality like? How do people feel about him?

Yv: He's highly respected. He's a leader, merchant, seaman. He's loving, but uh, I don't want to say stern. He's very straightforward in many ways. Things are to be done, and they get done.

M: What do other people call him? How is he known at this point?

Yv: The name Joseph is coming to me. I don't know if this is correct.
{*My consciousness is interfering with Yaakov's explanation by second-guessing. I'm not wanting to use previous info I have read, but it is a moot point because I actually do not recall it is Joseph of Arimathea until after the session.* ~~ *Justin*}

M: What do you call him?

Yv: Uncle.

M: What does your grandmother call him?

Yv: Joseph.

M: Thank you.

M: When you look at your grandmother and your uncle and their relationship...is there anything you can tell us about this?

Yv: She's a little woman but very strong. Very much a leader. He respects her very much and generally takes directions from her unless it's about the ship or some other aspect that is out of her purview.

M: So, he's your uncle. He is your mother's brother or your father's brother?

Yv: My mother's brother.

M: He is older than your mother, or younger?

Yv: Older.

M: What is his relationship like with your mother?

Yv: Protective, like an older brother. Sometimes almost like a father. He looks after all of us that way.

M: Are there any other siblings beside your uncle and your mother?

Yv: There are many, eight comes to mind but I'm not sure.

M: Thank you. Is there anything more about this scene or should we move forward in time?

Yv: Let's move forward. I want to get to the camp.

M: Let's move forward to the next important scene.

Yaakov is very excited, mirthful, breathy, almost on the verge of tears, he can barely contain himself. He sprints to his brother ahead of the group.

Yv: He's here! I see him. So good to see him!

M: Just enjoy that reunion.

Yv: We clasp and hug and look at each other and are walking with our arms around our shoulders. We are talking rapidly about what's going on. He wants to hear about the trip.

I want to hear about what he's been doing...there is too much talk all at once.

The village is there, they are greeting my uncle and my grandmother. Lots of talk, lots of voices, lots of excited voices, lots of greetings.

Yeshua and I are trying to move to the edge of the group so we can talk, but the grown-ups want his attention.

{As the villagers come out to greet our group, there is much joyous calling and laughter. Uncle and Grandmother know many of these people well. Yeshua and I try to stay on the periphery to talk but it is disrespectful to move away at this time. This is a summer camp for these people. ~~ Justin}

M: How old is Yeshua now?

Yv: Sixteen.

M: How does he look?

Yv: He's uh, slender build, but what you would call sort of a lanky musculature.

M: Do you two look alike?

Yv: It's hard for me to look at me, let me see...I think I'm a little...

M: Allow yourself the perception as if you look through his eyes, can you do that?

Yv: Birds' eye view: we're about the same height and build. I am a little stouter and muscular, he's a little more slender than I am. I am a little darker than he is. He's been living up in the north and his skin is lighter now.

{We are at the edge of camp, I see Yeshua and I am overcome with love and excitement. We embrace, laughing and smiling, looking at each other at arm's length, trying to walk to the edge of the gathering, arms over each other's shoulders. We are almost the same height, he is a little bit taller. He is more slender than I, I have been sailing and not as active for several weeks. Usually we walk so much and are so active we are both slender. I am darker-skinned with a youth's musculature. He is lighter, not having much sun living in this land. He wears his hair shoulder length, either loose or tied back with a leather thong as is the custom of these people. My hair is shorter. I am told much like Justin wears his hair now- but I have more-HA! ~~ Justin}

M: What is happening?

Yv: I'm just really happy to be with him. There's curiosity about the land and the camp and the people here. But mostly I'm happy to be with him right now. I want to hear about all the things he's been doing.
What he's been learning...to talk to the wind, the water, and the trees, the birds to sing...

M: That's what he's been doing?

Yv: Yes, to sing in a way, it's like commands but it's not commands. You work with the elements...REQUEST, request.

M: Request?

Yv: You're requesting, yes. You request their assistance in what you want to do. Like moving the big rocks, you sing, and you request.
Moving water.
Moving wind.
You request their help.
He's shaping. He's shaping a ball of light and energy between his hands. He's bouncing it back and forth, up and down.

M: And you can see it?

Yv: Yeah, it's almost like he's juggling it now. He's throwing it around in circles (laughter). Pretty cool!

M: Does he love sharing this with you?

Yv: Yes, he's real excited about it. There's other things he's doing he says he can't share, but these are things he can show me that he's been doing.

We're over by a stream and there's rocks and trees as we have this conversation, not far from the village, but far enough that we can talk.

He says the importance of the training is the importance of understanding how we are related to all of the world.

M: The natural world?

Yv: Yes.

We're a part of the life of this planet that we share with them. And we have the ability to use and abuse it. And he's being taught how to take care of and work with it for the sacredness of all beings.

M: How does Yaakov feel as you are hearing all this from him? How are you taking it in?

Yv: Serious, interested. The uh, interaction he has developed with nature is fascinating. He says he's been learning different ways of healing, too. Grandmother has always helped with healing. He says she learned some of that from here, some of it from her old country, some of it from home. She has a large wealth of knowledge. Herbs and remedies, energy of the body and herbs and remedies. Matching energies, understanding the energies of different plants, what's needed for the person that's sick or has a wound.

M: Has Yeshua been practicing this there?

Yv: Yes, when people are injured or sick in the village he goes with one of the elders and they teach him. We don't have these trees and plants. It's very, very green and wet here. It's very dry at home. We have trees and plants, but not like it is here. Everywhere you look it is green.

M: Are clothes different here than from home?

Yv: It's late spring here, early summer, a little chilly. We've been given some leather we're wearing over wool. We have long, uh, it's not a cloak, call them jackets, but not a jacket like in your time. So, like a long shirt, made of wool, usually cotton and flax at home, but wool here. And they've put leather over it to help with the dampness and rain. No rain today though.
We're chilled because we come from a warmer climate. It's not a particularly cold day, it's just not warm like it is back home.

M: Thank you. Would you like to stay here longer, or move ahead?

Yv: Move ahead.

M: What are you seeing and experiencing?

Yv: He and I are walking. The words "India and Nepal" come up.
We're young men, twenties, walking on another journey. This time together. Either where we are or where we are going. Oh-- we're in India going to Nepal. We're walking on foot. There are other people in the group, people carrying supplies.

M: Is there a sense of purpose on this trip?

Yv: Training and studying. We're always training and studying.

M: Are you and Yeshua training and studying the same things or different things?

Yv: Sometimes we study the same things and sometimes we're given different instructors for different things.

M: What can you share with us about the training?

Yv: We're taught what is known now as Martial Arts. A way to defend ourselves, a way to use energy. Ways, we're taught similar to scripture. They have books written like we do but it's a different language and they're teaching us- (pause to get the right word) BUDDHISM.

M: Can you give me some example of what you have learned?

Yv: Some phrase...I don't understand it.
Hare Krishna monta mema henan. (spelled phonetically)
Hare Krishna monta mema henan.
Hare Krishna monta mema henan.
I don't know what that means.
(Translated later by Aaron to mean "The God of love and compassion captures the heart.")
The teachings are all in a different language and different setting.
We are to respect and love each other and all those around us. And even though they are teaching us the martial arts, this defense, we're to be non-violent and passive. The teaching martial arts is more for discipline. Discipline of the body, discipline of the mind.

M: Does the martial arts have something to do with the energy as well?

Yv: Yes, I'm watching somebody moving light, sort of like Yeshua, but he had a ball of light. This is swirling light that he's harvesting from the world around him. He's gathering the energy around him.

{Yeshua with the Druids had a ball of light that was approximately grapefruit size and appeared solid which he was juggling. This light is energy being pulled from the world around and made visible in a swirling circle from the person's hands-a Tibetan man in monk's robes is standing. As he rotates his extended and slightly cupped hands and arms, he gathers energy and creates a circle of light with air inside, as if someone were drawing a circle of light around two feet in diameter. ~~ Justin}

M: You can actually see the energy?

Yv: Yes.

M: Is he a teacher?

Yv: He is an advanced student that is demonstrating what the teacher wants us to learn.

M: Have you and Yeshua been training in this very long? Can you do the same thing with the energy?

Yv: We are just beginners. I can move the energy a little. Yeshua is better at it, part of it's the training he had with the Druids. It comes more naturally.

M: And how do you each feel about learning this?

Yv: It's interesting to learn it. We're not quite sure of its use. But we trust that everything we're being taught is what we need to learn. We know there are...there is much work to be done in the near future as Yeshua goes forward to spread the Truth, and we don't know how each of these things we've been taught along the way are necessary.

M: And who sent you to this place?

Yv: Uncle, Mother, Father, Grandmother, they all agreed it was time for us to go here. Uncle's been here before. He has the contacts. That's how we get around. He has many financial resources. He either takes us, or makes sure that we have people to take us where we need to go with safe passage.

M: Are there others with you, or just the two of you?

Yv: There are other students, but they are from here. We are the only ones from our village. In this village they are very humble and quiet. We're at a monastery up in the mountains, and there's a village down below.
Nepal. There are snowcapped mountains that way. (Yaakov points to the NE) High, snowcapped mountains.

M: Are there only men at the monastery? Any women?

Yv: Yes, only when the villagers come up to bring items.
{Yes, there are only men. Yes, there are women when they come from the village to bring items. ~~ Justin}

M: Do they bring you food?

Yv: Yes, food and cloth.

M: Are you learning any other practices?

Yv: Sound, the use of sound. They have these bowls. Bowls and gongs. They use (these) to change the sound. Sometimes it's for different levels of meditation, sometimes it's for healing. But used inappropriately it can also cause pain. Gongs can be a weapon of sound.

M: Have you ever seen that done?

Yv: No, we're just simply warned to be respectful of these instruments and only use them as instructed.

M: Have they been welcoming to you there?

Yv: Yes, they know they're supposed to help us train.

M: Do you have a meditation practice there as well?

Yv: Yes, too many hours sometimes. Cold, stone floor. Sometimes you have a mat, but it's not comfortable. We're supposed to learn to go past that discomfort.
{We meditate frequently, daily, more than once a day frequently. Hard stone floors, sometimes a mat, but still hard stone floors. Hard on the knees, cold on the body. Part of meditation has been to escape the harsh sensations, going beyond the pain and discomfort. ~~ Justin}

M: How's that going?

Yv: We can do it. But it's not comfortable, it's not fun, but acknowledge it's what we need to do.

M: To go past the pain?

Yv: Right.

M: What helps with that?

Yv: Just knowing that you can. It's a state of mind. You move past the discomfort into the All Knowing, into the space. You let go of those human issues, human desires, physical body discomfort. You go past that, you let it fall away.
I'm not as interested as Yeshua. Yeshua, it seems more natural for him. I'm doing this because I need to, and I'm told to. But it's not as much of an interest.

M: What would you rather be doing?

Yv: I like the rituals at home. The chanting, the movement, thesong...what I grew up with. *{Yaakov is rocking his upper torso while sitting as he talks about this as if he was praying or reading the Torah in a traditional Jewish manner. ~~ Justin}*

I like the concepts they teach about respecting everyone and everything, treating each other well, no violence, the importance of nature.

But I like our chanting and rhythmic way when they read the Torah. That's comforting.

M: What language?

Yv: Hebrew.

M: What language are they speaking at the monastery?

Yv: Burmese.
{I did not know about the types of languages spoken now or then in this area of the world. Upon looking up the Burmese language, it was interesting to find out it is of the Sino-Tibetan language and included the geographic area of Nepal. ~~ Justin}

M: How does the communication work with language differences?

Yv: We have a translator and Yeshua is very good with languages, he picks it up easily.
{They speak Burmese. We speak Hebrew and Aramaic. Yeshua is good with languages and has learned many while traveling and studying. He can interact more easily with our instructors because of his gift for language. ~~ Justin}

M: Sounds like you are learning so very much there. Is there something you want to share with us, or is your inclination to move to a different time and space?

Yv: I'd like to move on. This was mainly to show us this highlight in time.

(We're) in India! There's a young boy running up to Yeshua, it's his son. We're headed back home.

M: What is his son's name? What does Yeshua call him?

Yv: Mikael? I don't know if that's correct. They call him something else in another language.

M: How do you feel about Yeshua's son?

Yv: He's cute.

M: How old?

Yv: Picture keeps shifting, three, four, five...difficult to tell.

M: What can you tell us?

Yv: I think the importance of this is he has a family here. It's uncomfortable for me because it's not someone from home. Well, it's a different culture, different religion. I know we've been trained in different cultures and religions for the last decade but it's sorta the expectation is that we will marry from our own people. This woman is not from our own people.

M: Can you describe her?

Yv: Dark skin, dark hair, intelligent, bright laughing eyes—she's got some kind of chain from her nose (left nostril) to the side of her face (ear). She's got these flowy bright clothes. She and Yeshua love each other very much.
{Research showed it is tradition in some Hindu cultures for a married woman to pierce her nostril, left in north, right in the south; it was also a part of medicine to help relieve childbirth pains. ~~ Justin}

M: Are there other children?

Yv: There is, or will be, another child, a girl child.

M: Are you in a relationship there?

Yv: There are many beautiful young women but the language and the culture is different and I'm not interested. I am here to study, to learn. I'm here to be with my brother.

M: Can you tell me more about what you are learning?

Yv: That was at the monastery (learning). We're on our way back home, now, passing through this area.

M: Do you know where she lives?

Yv: No.

M: Will she stay there?

Yv: Yes.

M: What is Yeshua's perspective of this woman and his child/children in India? What does he want us to know?

Yv: In our ways it is possible to have more than one spouse from the tribal histories of our people.

M: Is she his spouse?

Yv: No—she's a lover. Lover that he's been taught special skills with, so they're very close.

M: And she's his teacher of these special skills?

Yv: Yes.

M: Is Yaakov disapproving of this?

Yv: It's a mixture. Disapproving because it's not our ways from home, but it's part of his training. Maybe a little envious that he gets that training and I didn't. But I really don't want a family and children here, so that's ok.

M: Is he very open in telling you about this special training?

Yv: Something to do with light. Light and love.

M: Can you ask him about anything important for us to know about this?

Yv: It's sacred and not done irresponsibly.

M: How old are you now?

Yv: Twenty-three.

M: Yeshua?

Yv: Almost twenty-five. But I'm shown...ok. We were there for quite a while. So, like, twenty-eight for him, twenty-five, twenty-six...in our mid-twenties.

M: You were there together?

Yv: Yes, most of the time at the monastery. It's complete. — *{Signaling that all that is to be shared here is done and it is time to move on. ~~ Justin}*

M: Allow yourself to move to another time and space.

Yv: We will be going to a more intense time and our time tonight is done, to look at that another time.

M: With respect may we ask some questions?

Yv: Yes.

M: Ask the subconscious of Yaakov whether he and Yeshua have the same mother?

Yv: We have the same mother, but not the same father because Yeshua was light conceived like his children in India.

But Joseph's his father, anyway.

M: Joseph is Yaakov's father?

Yv: Joseph is a strong, kind, and loving man, father of all of us although as I said, Yeshua was light conceived so biologically he's not Joseph's.

M: What is your understanding that Yeshua is light conceived?

Yv: Directly from Creator, the divine light and love of life joined with our mother to create him in her womb.

M: Is this part of the special skills Yeshua is learning with his lover in India?

Yv: Yes.

M: Is there any more about that for now?

Yv: No.
{The concept of light conception is described in detail in the book, "Anna, Grandmother of Jesus," which explains the concept of the "virgin birth." ~~ Justin}

Day 3
May 26, 2017

Yaakov

Induction: they want to explain the remote-control thing of yesterday...

{A discussion takes place between myself and Maggie as spirit shows me what was meant. It is quite interesting that spirit wanted Maggie to give me the remote-control gift. Apparently, they had seen the Deep Spring IT staff using the remote the night before at the workshop about healing with Barbara and several spirit entities, the remote control allowed them to zoom the video camera in and out, changing focus of people and events. Evidently, the spirit helpers thought this remote-control concept would help me zoom in and out as I was Yaakov during the regressions. Maggie was hesitant to offer this to me, but did so on the repeated urging of spirit. Once it was offered, and we were able to figure out the intent, we found it to be very interesting how tuned in they are to our world as we do this work and want to help with its success. ~~ Justin}

The grove: Yeshua and a young boy of five or six (no identification), he wants to be there. He is going to watch.

I paused in the center of swirling light and found the cosmos swirling around me clockwise, right to left under my feet, over my head, passing through a round portal.

Arrival: *I am Yaakov.* There's a group of men sitting and talking on a low hillside. We've just left the road we are traveling on, going from one town to another. There are two women helping to serve us a meal, a snack during this break, Martha and Mary. They are with us today because it is a shorter trip.

M: What can you tell us about these two women? What is important about their presence?

Yv: They're part of our community, The Magdalene order that supports what Yeshua does.

M: In what way do they support what Yeshua does?

Yv: Spiritually, they have gifts of their own, things that they have been taught. On a day-to-day basis they often help with the needs of Yeshua or the men.

M: Are they related?

Yv: They are sisters.

M: Related to the men?

Yv: No.

M: Describe the Magdalene order.

Yv: Inner core of our village community which has been entrusted to knowledge about what Yeshua must do and various people have been assigned roles and given opportunities to train and study to fulfill these roles. All in support of getting the Truth out to the people.

M: Yaakov, are you aware of what your group role is?

Yv: All the details haven't been explained yet. I am friend and support for my brother. And, I need to be aware of certain aspects of the training, which I'll be told later how they fit with what I need to do.

M: How do you feel about this role that you have?

Yv: Well, I love my brother as my brother, but I also honor and respect him for the task he's been given and accepted; it's a little difficult at times. I am not really interested in the things they want me to learn, or I am interested and they're difficult to learn.

M: Can you give us an example?

Yv: Control of the physical body to almost death, but not death.

M: Is that one that is difficult, or one you're not interested in?

Yv: I have a cerebral interest in it, it's very difficult. It's not one I want to practice. I know it's important for Yeshua.

M: Are you still in the group of men?

Yv: Yes, I'm off to the side a little, watching.

M: What else is important for you to share about this scene?

Yv: These are the men later who are termed "disciples/apostles." A mixture of men, most without any spiritual or religious training beyond what they get from the rabbis. They don't... they're not a part of the Magdalene order so they have a different perspective than what we do and often don't understand what Yeshua's trying to explain.

M: What brings this group of men together today?

Yv: Following him, supporting him. Trying to learn what he is teaching. *One of the* important messages is women are just as important for this as men. They often traveled with us in support.

M: How are the men receiving their message?

Yv: Most of the men are seeing them just as they would their sisters, their mothers, or their wives, just taking care of them.

M: Is this message about women radical?

Yv: Yes, and not really accepted by many of them.

M: How do you, Yaakov, feel about this?

Yv: I feel somewhat of an outsider because they don't understand. I know they want to understand, but I feel a little of an outsider. I just sit quietly back and let Yeshua do what he needs to do.

M: And how do you feel about the message he is sharing about women being just as important?

Yv: That's the way I've grown up. Grandmother was a strong leader...um...Mother's main goal was to make sure we were loved and nurtured; there were many children. She helped with the education, but a large component was left to Grandmother.

M: So, there is a belief you have grown up with, is it a part of the Magdalene order?

Yv: Yes, they are all a part of that and Yeshua and the Truth. The message that needs to go out. The village is comprised of those that follow the Essene way, but not all of those are a part of the Magdalene way, it's an inner circle.

M: Explain what you mean by the Essene way.

Yv: The Essene way is different from the mainstream Jewish religion, Judaism. We don't use the same hierarchy or priests and Sanhedrin and such. We believe that men and women should be equally educated and equally respected. There are different roles for different people, but they don't necessarily have to be based upon sex. Knowledge is very important, treating each other with love and respect, eating wholesome nutritious foods...

M: You mentioned feeling like you are an outsider in this scene.

Yv: Yes.

M: Is there something that you're feeling sad about?

Yv: Yeshua says it's important to have these men learn the message as he goes from town to town bringing the message. There are those who will be hearing it for the first time and it's all new. These men will comprise a group that will hear it over and over and learn it better. More, um, the goal is for them to understand the message better, and support the message he is trying to bring. So, as they go from town to town they can help teach, or when they are off on their own they can help teach. But I'm frustrated because they don't have the same knowledge and learning we have had all our lives, and they have different perspectives, they're having difficulty understanding and learning and sometimes their interpretations of the message are different than what is intended.

M: Is this what frustrates you?

Yv: Yes.

M: Do you ever participate in the teaching?

Yv: Sometimes I help. But they really want to hear from him, so I stay in the background as support.

M: Does he share your frustration of the men not getting the message correctly?

Yv: Sometimes, but, he's (laugh and smile) ...Yeshua is always optimistic and very loving. He has faith. Faith that they will learn enough. But yes, where he tries to teach, and it seems like they're not able to understand, or he's teaching the same thing over and over and they still don't understand, it can be frustrating. And they still tend to treat the women as less than equal even though he reminds them--if they're talking in a tone, or commanding in a way, he'll gently redirect them.

M: As you speak, I get a strong sense that getting the message right is very important, almost a sense of urgency. Is that right?

Yv: I don't know about a sense of urgency, but we need to get it right. That's the whole point of what we're doing, is to get it right. To give the message of Truth.

M: Is there anything that comes to mind as an example of these men or others not quite getting it right or having a distortion about what he's teaching?

Yv: The prodigal son. We are all prodigal sons and daughters. We have felt separated from our Father and Creator and with shame and feelings of unworthiness. We seek his love and forgiveness. But there needs be no shame or unworthiness. We are all worthy. We are all loved unconditionally.

They see it as very concrete as one bad son went off and came back and his father gave him everything--and why should this happen? But that is not the message. It's about all of us.

M: Thank you so much for that clarification. Is there anything else about this scene that seems important to share at this time? Relationship with Yeshua? Group of men? Women?

Yv: I love my brother, and I'm trying so hard to do the best job I can to help support him. I'm feeling a little lost. Because I don't understand exactly yet what I'm going to do other than be by his side. Just feeling a little lost and outside trying to just be loving and supportive. A little anxious, maybe.

M: Do you have any support besides Yeshua when you are feeling these things? Do you have any other family of your own?

Yv: No, I'm single and have devoted my time to my role helping Yeshua.

M: Is there more or would you like to move on?

Yv: Yeshua and I are very close as brothers and comrades. We've done a lot of things together and he's always very loving. As we go forward in this process, part of my feelings of loss and being an outsider is when I ask my grandmother, "What am I to do? Why am I learning this?"
"You'll be told, in time you"ll be told."
It's a bit..., because I've been hearing that for so long, it feels a bit dismissive. As an adult I should be able to know.

M: Do you share these feelings with Yeshua?

Yv: Yes, and he's just loving. He doesn't know the exact reason for my role either, yet. Says we just need to trust. Trust it will be revealed and unfold as it needs to unfold and keep doing what we've been taught.

M: You and Yeshua are a part of the Magdalene order, do you have any practices or rituals that you participate in regularly that connect you to Creator, Source of All That Is?

Yv: Regular prayer and meditation, cleansing.

M: Can you describe for us what that looks like?

Yv: It can vary, but:

Creator of all there is and all there ever was and all there ever will be
We thank you for your everlasting love and light

We ask for your continued love and light and guidance throughout our day

Knowing we honor you, and honor ourselves in the highest way possible.

M: Thank you, I can really feel that strong powerful connection. Is there more you can say about these practices?

Yv: We're taught that the Source of all living things, our entire universe, which by our knowledge is somewhat limited...Jerusalem, the sea, the lands we've traveled to...we know there is more, but we don't have a concrete knowledge of what that is. But we accept that it's all created by the Source of Unconditional Love and Light and all for a reason.

M: For a reason?

Yv: Yes, it's not just random. It's all been planned and all for a reason. Expansion of the Source Love and Light. Out of love these things are created and out of love they are experienced.

M: Are you still in the group of men?

Yv: They're over at the hillside. I'm under a tree. In listening distance, but I'm not paying attention.

M: Do you as Yaakov have any like-minded friends or colleagues that really understand the message the way you do?

Yv: Mary is probably the only one who really understands as well as Yeshua and I.

M: Can you tell us about Mary, can you describe her? How do you /Yeshua feel about her?

Yv: Mary is like a sister to me. She's bright, kind, beautiful, strives to please Yeshua. She loves him very much.

M: How does Yeshua feel about her?

Yv: He loves her, but, uh, his work takes precedence.

M: Does he love her the same way he loves everyone, the same way he loves you?

Yv: She's special in his heart. I love and respect her, not in a romantic way. I'm not interested in that way.

M: Thank you so much. Any more to discuss or are you inclined to move to a different space and time?

Yv: He's showing me that, uh, because you ask about Mary, they have walked off to the hillside to be by themselves. He takes her hand in his and takes one of her hands to rub up against his cheek as he looks at her with love and smiles.

The work that they do is so important and intense. He doesn't feel that he could be a responsible husband to her. He already has another wife, and children from his Indian lover and, uh, he doesn't see them very often as it is. If they were to marry and have children, she would be at home as well and not with him. So, this way he loves her, and she's near him helping to optimize his success, but he doesn't feel a burden of responsibility towards her. Does that make sense?

M: Anything else?

Yv: There are small tears in her eyes as she loves him and understands and accepts this role with a very high honor and respect. In her own way, a partner to him to maximize their success in what they need to accomplish.

M: Is there anything she would like to share with us from her perspective, offer her a voice.

Ma: This is Mary (voice changes to a higher pitch).

I so love Yeshua and it is my highest honor to help and support him. As Yaakov explained, if we were to be married, I would have to stay at home with children. This way I am on the road traveling with him and the men. Helping and tending and teaching in a way I wouldn't be able to otherwise. I accept this as a very high honor to be able to help him and teach the Truth. The men don't want to listen to me, but the women do. And as women we're able to circulate amongst the women in villages we're at. A group with women is less threatening to the villagers as well. As a group of men only, they could be bandits, or otherwise threatening to the community. But when women travel with them it's less threatening. We visit with the other women, find where to get food, water, lodging. It's much easier.

M: Mary, thank you, I get a sense you have a special role in this teaching of this message. What is your understanding of the role?

Ma: Like all of us in the Magdalene order, we've been raised from children to understand the Truth. And those of us that were interested had additional trainings. Some us excelled and some of us chose not to finish pursuing those. I was very good at many. Martha lost interest and that's not anything negative to her.

M: Explain what you were very good at.

Ma: Learning and understanding.

M: Are those special skills, concepts?

Ma: The Truth, some healing, love, in the bigger context. That's all I can say right now.

M: Thank you so much. Much gratitude and love to you.

Ma: And to you, thank you.

M: Let me know if someone else wants to step forward and speak from their perspective.

JA: This is Joseph (in a clear, strong loud voice of authority)

The children have been trained as we have been led, each to their own skills and interest. None are required to do that which they are not interested in or willing to do. It's all by choice.

M: Thank you, Joseph. What is your role?

JA: I am uncle, I am brother to Anna. We have been trained in many, many skills and methods to support the Truth. As you know Egypt, the north, India as well as our traditional Jewish ways...we take which is best for propagating the Truth. We teach our children, so that they may teach theirs, all as an expression of the Creative Source of Unconditional Love. But mainly I wanted to emphasize that everyone has the opportunity to learn, not only those that wish to go forward in the training.

M: It seems you are letting us know that no one is forced to do anything against their will. Is that right?

JA: Yes.

M: And everyone is allowed to do that which suits their abilities.

JA: Yes, not everyone is learning the same things.

M: Thank you.

JA: And some are choosing not to learn more specialized roles, as Martha chose not to. But her love and support are accepted and appreciated.

M: I get a sense from what you are saying, that each member of the community is valued for what they have to offer and how they choose to assist. Is that right?

JA: Yes, thank you for understanding.

M: Can you clarify your relation? Did you say you are brother to Anna?

JA: Yes, relation to Mary, Yeshua's mother. Uncle.

M: Is there someone else who wants to share and step forward with a sense of what is right to do at this time? Anything Yeshua wants us to know right now?
Yaakov, can you tell us what you are feeling/seeing?

Yv: I am reviewing the relationship of Joseph. Marianna is Mother. Joseph is her brother. Sometimes he referred to her as Mary, sometimes Anna, little Anna.

M: He was not speaking about Yeshua and Yaakov's grandmother?

Yv: Correct.

M: His mother is named...

Yv: Anna.

M: His sister is named Mary.

Yv: Yes.

M: Thank you.

Anything else you would like to share at this time that's important? Can we ask Yaakov what he feels is right to him at this time?

Yv: *To rest.*

Day 3
May 26, 2017

Ascension

Yv: I am in the tomb and I am trying to figure out what we are doing.

M: In THE tomb?

Yv: In a tomb. Yeshua is laid out under cloths.

M: Is this Yaakov?

Yv: It is.

M: Can you describe what you are seeing and feeling?

Yv: It's sundown on Sabbath. Yeshua has been carried into the tomb, he is lying with his head toward the opening, feet over here. I am on this side of him (*his head to my left, feet to right, I am on the right side of him*) and over there is Mary Magdalene (*on his left side by his shoulder*) and over there is Grandmother (*on his left side by his feet*). We are holding space for him in a triangulation pattern.

M: Holding space in a what pattern?

Yv: Triangulation pattern. Everyone else, except the family, thinks that he's dead. He's using the teaching and the skills to bring down his breathing and his heart rate. He can breathe without using his chest. He can lower his heart rate enough to beat so that when someone checks it, he can stop it temporarily and resume it when they leave. When someone checks on him it appears that he is dead. But this is a critical time because if he (*his body*) actually dies, his spirit will leave like everyone else's. The goal is to ascend, to bring his body and his spirit together at a higher frequency so that the body leaves with spirit. Joseph, our uncle, is in the background trying to make sure that everything is readied.

M: You, Mary and your grandmother are holding space in a triangulation pattern...can you describe what it is that you are doing? What it means by holding space?

Yv: We each have a crystal, we're praying, we're connecting to the eternal Source. Protecting Yeshua, his spirit, his body, his energy from any outside influence.

M: How do the crystals help?

Yv: They magnify our energy and the energy from the Source to help create this perimeter of protection for him. And it...I think he draws on some of the energy as well. But our main job is to hold this space in the energy so that he is protected, and he can do whatever he needs to do.

M: I get a sense the energy above is very important too.

Yv: Yes.

M: Explain that.

Yv: It's creative Source, it's Unconditional Love, it's the Source of all life and it needs to be here to protect from anything that might not um.... might be more...for lack of a better word, negative...that might want to interfere with what he needs to do as opposed to drawing upon that energy and love that supports what he needs to do. And he is using that unconditional love and the life force to help keep him alive and bring him up...bring his frequency up.

M: How are you feeling now, Yaakov?

Yv: (*Sigh, breath out*)...I don't want to make any mistakes, any mistakes and he'll die.

M: Do you feel well prepared and ready for this challenge?

Yv: I am prepared. My love for him and my sense of responsibility to him, my family, the Truth, it's all a part of, all a part of this.

M: So, a sense of responsibility...a sense of great responsibility with no room for mistakes or errors...

Yv: Oh, yes.

M: Others in your triangular think the same?

Yv: They do. Grandmother, who has more experience, is more confident. Right now there is a little bit of concern on her part that either Mary or I will falter, but not because we don't want to do what we need to do, just because of lack of experience. We've practiced, but y'know, this is the final exam.

M: Yes, and when you've practiced in the past did you know what the final exam would be?

Yv: Not until recently. Grandmother explained that there would be times that she would go into "suspension," she's much older than she appears. And these were some of the techniques that were used. So, we thought, we were just being trained in those ways for that information to be used later if we wanted to.

M: At what point did you learn this would be used with your brother, Yeshua?

Yv: When they took him from the garden, Grandmother explained that the time was now. That if...

M: What will be important for us to know about these events leading up to where we are now in the tomb?

Yv: I'm trying to determine if I was at what they call the "Last Supper." I think I was in and out attending to something that needed to be done.

M: Can you take a peek at that scene they call the Last Supper from whatever viewpoint--Yaakov's, or a bird's eye view from above--and tell us what might be important for us to know?

Yv: Yes, Mary was there. And a few others helping to serve and tend, the usual "disciples" were there.

M: The usual disciples?

Yv: Yes, he was trying to make them understand without telling them directly.

M: What did he want them to understand?

Yv: That even when he is no longer with them, he has taught them what they need to know to pass on the information, pass on the Truth. And that is their role. That's why they've been with him all this time, to learn, and understand, and be able to pass on the Truth. And that even when he is not there, by simply seeing their daily wine and bread, they can remember his words. That was the impact and importance of "this bread is my body and this wine is my blood." It's just remembering him as they went through their daily routines. Eating is one of those daily routines.

M: So, what you're saying is he wanted them to remember him daily?

Yv: To remember yes, not him as a man, but him as the message, the Truth. What he's taught them and the love, the Unconditional Love that he shares with everyone. And to go forth in that way, with Unconditional Love and Truth.

M: What's your understanding as Yaakov what he means by Truth?

Yv: There is one Creator. A creative Source of Unconditional Love. We are to be a part of that love, feeling it, knowing that we are always loved and sharing that love with each other. Treating each other with the love and respect that one would have and use in the setting of Unconditional Love.

M: As you focus in and zoom in on that scene, can you see Yeshua?

Yv: Yes, I've been watching him as we've talked.

M: Is your understanding that he knows what will transpire at this point?

Yv: He has an idea, but the details remain to be seen. Futures can always change.

M: Can you see yourself, Yaakov, in the scene?

Yv: Seems as if I am coming in and out. I'm checking on things and then going away to do something else, and then I check on them again.

M: Is there anything Yeshua wants us to know before we leave the scene?

Yv: The controversy about Judas has been discussed.

M: Amongst you?

Yv: Amongst YOU.

M: Yes, would you like to clarify that?

Yv: He did as Yeshua asked without fully understanding the impact.

M: Yeshua asked him to do what he did?

Yv: Yes, take the money and when you see me in the garden, greet me as you normally would. He did not know that I would be arrested and tortured and killed.

M: He did not know that Yeshua would be arrested and tortured and killed?

Yv: Yes.

M: So, it is important for us to know he (Judas) didn't know what he was doing, he was doing what he was told?

Yv: Yes. He was confused as to why he was given those instructions, but he obeyed. There were things...

Ya: This is Yeshua... (*stronger, clearer voice*).

There are things written in scriptures of old. That there would be a one who would come to speak the Truth, a Messiah. And he would be known by these acts. There were certain things that needed to be done in certain manner in order to be recognized as "one who speaks the Truth." There were many in that day and age claimed to be the Messiah. I did not claim to be "the Messiah." People put that name on me, that label on me. I was the "messenger of Truth." But in order for people to understand they were to listen to this message and not the other messages, certain acts of scripture needed to be fulfilled. Riding in with the donkey on Palm Sunday, and other things...do you understand?

M: I think. Can you explain how it is to be the messenger than the Messiah?

Ya: They are one and the same. I am saying I didn't call myself the Messiah during those times. My title was "the messenger of Truth." That's what I agreed to be, the messenger of Truth. It is labeled Messiah in the scripture. Do you see the difference?

M: Other people labeled you, it wasn't a self-identity that you had.

Ya: Correct. I understand it to be the same, but I didn't call myself the Messiah. Like others who would say "I am the Messiah; no, I am the Messiah. No, I am the Messiah." (*Different voice changes intonating different people claiming to be the Messiah*). I was the Messenger of Truth. In order to know which Truth was to be listened to, those acts had to be completed and the ascension needed to be completed.

M: The ascension needed to be completed?

Ya: If I just died like anybody else, what would be the difference?

M: So, it needed to be different for the message to stand out, is that what you are saying?

Ya: Yes, to say THIS is the one we need to listen to. And these are the possibilities: to love unconditionally; to treat each other with love; to have a direct connection with our Father-Creative Source, Creative Source of All.

M: Thank you, Yeshua. What other misunderstandings do you want to clear up at this time?

Ya: Grandmother has written a lot. There's controversy about Mary, Mary Magdalene, my beloved. Beautiful, sincere woman, who put her own wants and desires aside to love me and love our Father, and help fulfill the work that needed to be done. Never a harlot, never a whore. I came to her first (*after the ascension*) because she is my beloved and I wanted to make sure that she knew that all the work that she had done had been successfully completed. (*Yeshua chokes with tears while saying "successfully completed"*) I thanked her.

M: You went to her after they tried to kill you?

Ya: After I ascended. She...maybe you aren't aware of the story. She came to check on me in the morning. When they left that night, after sunset, I was breathing on my own in the tomb. So, when she came back the next morning and the rock was rolled away and there was no body, she panicked. She thought somebody had stolen me. So, I showed her myself in my higher frequency as I was ascending to thank and reassure her.

M: Part of the story is she didn't recognize you, is that accurate?

Ya: Well, how easy is it for you to recognize something that is not solid?

M: You needed to show yourself to her. What can you tell us about your brother, Yaakov?

Ya: Yaakov is a sweet man, very serious. Totally dedicated to his responsibility, to me, the Message, the process... to the exclusion of almost all else. I love him greatly. And I know he struggled after I left, that was a part of his journey to go forward with the Message and the Truth after I was gone. I had other things to do.

M: Other things to do. Tell us about his responsibility to carry the Message forward.

Ya: It was now up to him to take the Message of the Truth forward, as you say, and try to maintain its integrity. As much as I tried to teach the disciples and others that have heard my words, there remained much confusion. Changes in interpretation, changes in perspective... Yaakov tried valiantly to maintain, he DID maintain the Message. And he would try to correct. He's a loving, quiet man, up against very vocal Peter and Paul and others who meant well and tried to... they were sincere in their words and they thought it was Truth--it was close, but not the same. So, it was difficult for Yaakov. Especially he would ask me, "You're still around! Why don't you come and clarify for the people? Let them know." I would explain, I had already done that. I'd already done my part. I had other things to do now.

M: Can you tell us about the other things you had to do?

Ya: Working with other Masters; trying to change the vibrations, the frequencies; learning more for myself; always working with other Masters to develop ways to teach, teach those who could be listening. Those who have ears to hear, let them hear.

M: These other Masters you were working with, did they have names we might recognize?

Ya: Yes, but Anna has already talked about those and I don't want to reiterate that.

M: Could we ask you, Yeshua, while you're here, to understand better the dynamics between your brother Yaakov, and Peter and Paul? And the church they were developing? Or is that best for another time?

Ya: Our intent was to spread the Truth, spread the word, and as people would come to understand the concept of unconditional love and practice, that they would become enlightened--higher light frequency--and that would spread from person to person, as more were taught, more would learn, more would understand. But human... human emotion, human thoughts are so complex...there were changes in the message and changes in the practice, that led to arguments and confusion, to where the simple message of truth and love has been convoluted and changed and made very complicated. And I was a messenger. I'm not God, I'm not our Father. I'm not the original Source of creation and unconditional love. We are ALL part of that, we're ALL part of that divinity and yet I am singled out, that wasn't the intent. I am a way, if you follow what I've taught you will find your way to unconditional love and happiness. But I'm not the ONLY way. There are other Masters who have given similar messages, just different words, but the message is the same. The whole goal is to learn and practice unconditional love for yourself, for those close to you, for those you don't even know, for those who are hurting, for those who are lost, all of us.

M: Is there a practice or way you can suggest to do that?

Ya: I have spoken many times about that. Learning to love oneself, we're here to learn and grow, to not demean and not hate. I know it is difficult with the complexity of emotion, with the complexity of cultures, and different peoples living on this Earth. It can be done. The other night I gave further explanation about the Lord's Prayer.* Look at these words, look at the explanations:
*5-24-17. Deep Springs Center Healing Workshop can be found in its entirety on the DSC website and on YouTube.

Yeshua talks:

Let us begin with a simple prayer that I think all of you know. You know "**The Lord's Prayer**," as being my words. "When you pray, pray this way." What did I mean by these words? Let's take it a piece at a time, because I think this foundation is vital to your understanding of everything else we will discuss today.

"Our Father/Mother/Divine Creator, the Source of all that is, we praise Thy name."

Now, the Divine Creator— co-Creator with you; the source of light and love, does not need your praise. There's no ego there. Why would it seek praise? The praise is for you. When you praise, you raise your vibration. You come up to a higher place of love and begin to know who you truly are. "We praise your name." -- whatever name you give, and each tradition gives its own name. There is one God/Goddess/Divinity, many names. I love you. I cherish you and all that you have created.

"Thy kingdom come; Thy will be done."

In other words, may this light and love that you are be found everywhere. And may I of my own free will be a part of creating that light and love throughout all the universes, all the galaxies, everywhere. I am light, I am love; therefore, I am created in Thine image, I am light and love, and I choose to be a part of the co-creation on this heavy density planet. "Thy kingdom come." Thy will of Love everywhere and in everything. The Knowing of that love in everything. "Thy will be done."

"Give us this day our daily bread."

Is anybody here hungry? Do you need bread? What do you need? Do you need Light and love? What truly nourishes you? I think we can find some bread in the kitchen, if anyone needs it. But I doubt that's what you truly need. If it is what you need, of course we'll make sure it's available to you. But the essence, light, high vibration, love; that is what we ask. "Give us this day our daily bread."

"And forgive us our trespasses."

That's a harder one. If you know yourself to be light and always act in accordance with that light, then there are no so-called trespasses. But coming into this heavy density planet you forget who you are, and you cease to know yourself as light and as love. And then you act in antithesis to the core of your being, which is light and love. You act in service to self instead of service to all beings because you have slipped into the illusion of separation.

We ask forgiveness for that, that which shaped us, shaped us with free will and the possibility to hold to that true light or to slip into distortion. When you slip into distortion, you suffer. When you suffer, and you are paying attention, it helps you learn not to slip into the distortion of separation but to hold the space of love.

We ask forgiveness, we ask compassion for ourselves and all beings who, because of the humanness and living on this heavy density planet, do slip into distortion, do transgress against the illusory other, which is really the self. Because when I harm another, I harm myself.

"and help us to forgive those who trespass against us."

To see that they have also slipped into the illusion of separation, and out of that illusion have acted and spoken in ways that do harm. Each time we say, "I hold you in my heart," seeing the pain that creates the distortion of separation, we forgive. And in forgiving others, we forgive ourselves.

"Lead us not into temptation."

Lead us not into the paths that the separated ego would walk, but help us to know our innate connection with God/Goddess/All That Is.

"Deliver us from evil."

What is evil? How can anything be evil if God has created everything? On the ultimate level, there is no evil. On the relative level, we slip into the ego self, into the stories. Deliver us from, let us say from slipping into the illusion of separation. That's my best definition of evil: to become caught in the illusion of separation. "Deliver us from evil."

"For Thine is the kingdom, the power and the glory."
The one God/Goddess/Infinite Creator, the heart of love, it is that, the divine essence, that we adore and with which we come to know in non-duality.

Ya: Look to those around you who are teaching in fashion similar to mine. Barbara and Aaron, Justin and Tavis (a member of Deep Spring community, presently President of the Board), and many others who are faithful to the Message. Look to those without ego that truly just want to teach about unconditional love and light. Darkness is only the absence of light. Bring the light forward.

M: Thank you so much, is there anything else you want to share at this time?

Ya: No.

Large sigh, loud voice:
P: This is Peter!

M: Thank you for coming, Peter.

P: I feel like I'm getting a bad rap. But I did the best I could, the way that I understood. I honored and loved Yeshua as my teacher, my leader. I just wanted to raise him up to the highest point possible. So people would listen and follow in his way.

M: What's the bad rap you'd like to correct?

P: That I didn't understand in the way that I should have, or I needed to. I had a limited education, a different perspective and a different way of growing up. I tried to understand the best I could.

M: What did you see your role as being?

P: As all of us to take that Message forward. I happened to be a little more outspoken, a little more tenacious about what I thought was the right way, and I became a leader, founded the church.

M: Out of love for Yeshua?

P: Yes.

M: And you did the best you could?

P: Yes, I did.

M: What was your dynamic with Yaakov?

P: Strained. He was always a part of Yeshua's life, but always on the side supporting and loving, but quiet and in truth, we didn't really want to listen to what he had to say. He wasn't "The Chosen One," it was Yeshua. I know now that he knew, he knew what the Truth was. He wasn't as articulate, but he knew.

M: You did the best you could with leadership, and leadership is challenging. What were the challenges you faced?

P: Trying not to be killed by the Romans, for one!

M: That's a big challenge!

P: I wasn't part of the Jewish community, but the Sanhedrin, their leaders, they weren't happy either. People of my community, some had listened and heard Yeshua and wanted to understand; they did understand some. They wanted to hear more. There were others that didn't believe at all, just wanted to ridicule and blame.

M: Many challenges. Are there any you can tell us about that were of like mind with you, working for the same purpose?

P: Many of the disciples who had been with me when we were with Yeshua, but they tended to spread out in order to spread the Message, so they weren't right with me. In order to reach larger populations, we would spread out to try to do the work. Do the work without getting killed, by one faction or another.

M: How out in the open versus how secret did you have to be to do the work, to avoid being killed?

P: Well, most of the time we still met privately. Only on occasion when we knew we would be in a group of followers of like mind that we could be a little more open. We were always cautious. That's all.

M: Whoever has work to convey at this time, come forward.

Yv: This is Yaakov. At first, Peter and I tried to work together. But, we never worked well together in the past. It's not easy to work together. I was from Jewish, and especially an Essene role, and he was from a Gentile role. And we decided we needed to serve those populations separately. But, as he said, there were many, many challenges, non-believers, some were violent, those in the Jewish and Roman hierarchy that did not want it perpetuated and wanted to squelch Yeshua's influence.

M: Is there more about your relationship with Peter, or other disciples?

Yv: Wait, wait, wait.
?: A message about Caiaphas. Caiaphas was head, one of the heads of the Sanhedrin. He was fearful in many aspects, angry in others. Who was this upstart, Yeshua? He was raised in our communities, taught as a rabbi and leader, who now turns against us in our ways. On the other hand, what if he is right? What if we're wrong? What's going to happen to me? My way of life, my standing in the community? What's going to happen to me as far as my spirit if I'm wrong in the way that I've been practicing and praying and being? How am I going to explain this to the people? To the leaders? This is all just too much. We can't have him disrupting everything: our way of life, our way of prayer, our way of living. Those were the thoughts going through the mind of Caiaphas and it was out of desperation that he felt he needed to eliminate Yeshua's influence.

M: Is it correct he tried many times and, in many ways, to end Yeshua's life?

?: Oh, he tried to silence him, ignoring him, calling him out, challenging him--it didn't ever stop Yeshua. And so finally there was the opportunity to end his speaking forever.

M: What did he choose to do?

?: Tried to hand it off to the Romans to take care of so he wouldn't be responsible, but they gave it back to him. So, then he tried to hand it off to the people. He didn't want to look like he was responsible, but ultimately it was his responsibility.

M: Does he take responsibility now?

?: He knows it was his doing, he manipulated it, he knows.

M: Is this Yaakov telling us about it?

Yv: Appears to be a mixture--sort of a Knowing. Not any one person speaking right now.

Sigh, voice change
Speaks quickly and with confidence

I am: Fear, you see what fear does?

He was fearful, he made decisions based upon fear instead of love.

If we can make decisions based upon love instead of fear, people say it's lots of other emotions, but it all boils down to fear. If you are angry, why are you angry? Because you are often fearful of something. How someone's going to make you feel. Someone's going to do something, or do something you don't want them to do. Shame is fear, it all boils down to fear. A spectrum, love--fear. You can choose. Love or Fear.

Choose love.

M: Who is speaking now?

I am: The [Knowing], the "I am."
{In the review section you will read more about this guest who initially called himself "the knowing" and then asked this to be changed to "I am." ~~ Justin}

M: It's so clear. Thank you. What else?

I am: What else is there?

M: More love.

I am: Love. That's what it is. Love.
    Always choose love.
{very long pause}

I am: So simple--hmmm, yet so difficult.

M: So simple, it brings tears to my eyes.

I am: That means you feel it. That's good.

M: Can you speak about Yeshua's intent?

I am: Yes.

Yeshua so loved, they have used that term before, that he so loved the world. He came, and he was the messenger. He knew it would be difficult. Person after person, time after time, he has extended his love and his hands, and he continues to do that. Whatever you need, call upon me in the depths of despair, fear, sadness, I offer you love. Come feel the love. Come be a part of my Father and myself. It's always love. He didn't die for anybody's sins, he wasn't the scapegoat that took on all the sins, he was the messenger. The messenger of Truth and love. Do these things as I do. LOVE as I do. THAT was his message.

M: And the message got distorted, obviously.

I am: Yes.

M: Sin was inserted in there.

I am: Yes, we make mistakes. That's part of why we're here to learn and grow. You can't learn if all you do is the same thing over and over correctly. On the other side of the veil, intellectually you learn but over there you don't have to ...you are not challenged! So, you come here, you get challenged. You have to practice what you've learned. Just like anyone else, you learn about it, you read about it, someone teaches you, you learn a new skill, and then you have to go DO it!

M: Making mistakes of being imperfect.

I am: Exactly. You're here in order to do it and to practice it. To REALLY learn it. You're being challenged to learn those new skills of unconditional love and working through the fear, the anger, the sadness, whatever that emotion is that you experience here. If you don't learn to work through those, and come to love, you haven't learned it. Does that make sense?

M: You have to learn it to get the lesson.

I am: Yes! You get to...you get an OPPORTUNITY to learn it. That's what this is--opportunity to learn. An opportunity to practice it. So that you can go on and share that unconditional love, that co-creation, and others around you can learn it as well. If you're practicing love, others can learn that. If you're practicing hate and anger and all those other emotions, that's what people will learn as well. So, it's just a matter of what you're going to teach. What are you going to teach? What are you going to learn? Those around you are going to learn whatever you're teaching. So, it's your choice. What do you want to teach?

M: If it's not about sin, where does forgiveness come in?

I am: Recognizing that we're all on the same boat (Earth). We're all on the same journey. Trying to learn, taking those opportunities, trying to learn to practice that love. And when somebody doesn't get it right, when they do something that's harmful to you, you have to acknowledge that they didn't get it right. You have no control over them. And the same when we don't get it right. Because what happens if you don't forgive yourself? You feel guilt, you feel shame, you get fear about doing it right the next time. "Oh, I can't do it right, so why even try. I'll just keep doing it wrong." You go down that path, less and less light, more darkness.

M: Seems from your perspective, we're so slow to learn.

I am: I don't put a value on it. You learn when you learn, it takes as long as necessary. The ultimate goal, once it's reached, that's what's important. What you can learn along the way, you also learn compassion, which is part of love--right? Compassion for yourself, compassion for others. Lift them up, lift yourself up. The more light you give, the more love you give, the more likely the next choice will be in love.

M: Is that spoken from the [Knowing] "I am?"

I am: Yes.

M: Thank you.

I am: It's nothing new, nothing new.

M: I'd like to ask Yaakov if there is more he would like to share today?

(Sigh, voice change. Quieter, slower voice, as if trying to find words.)

Yv: It was my deepest honor to be a part of, to live my life and be a part of the Plan, Message of Truth. There was frustration as already talked about. Trying to have the integrity and speak the Truth, teach, and all the challenges and frustrations we had to do that. And there were times it seemed it would just be easier if Yeshua was there to speak instead of me.

M: You must have missed him so much.

Yv: Yeah. And sometimes I would get angry that, "You just ascended. You're around. I know you're around. I see you! You come and visit. YOU talk to them!" But I also understand that he **did** talk. You know, he spent three years talking and teaching and traveling. He fulfilled his part. It's important the other things he's doing. I understood that.

M: So, you knew he was around. Were you still in communication with him after he ascended?

Yv: Yes, sometimes he would visit. He'd visit us.

M: How could you see him?

Yv: Um, he got to a point with his frequency, he could control it so sometimes he was more solid and sometimes less. Less solid allowed him to travel, and then more solid he could interact with me or somebody else. He would make a point to visit me or the family. Knowing that he could make himself visible, and make himself heard, especially initially, that was difficult.

M: Yes, it put a lot on you.

Yv: Yes.

M: Would you like to say more about that at this time?

Yv: No, I think that says it. Just, we all did the best we could in the situation. And my role after the ascension was to continue to try to spread the word of the Truth. We did the best we could.

M: And from where you are now, can you see how important and how successful your role was?

Yv: Initially in the tomb...?
{*Yaakov started to say something, then changed his response.* ~~ *Justin*}

Yv: Hmm, yes, I'm so very thankful we were successful.

M: You had a lot of work. Took on a lot of responsibility for that very important role.

Yv: Well, from a personal level also, he was my **brother**, I didn't want him to die! There's a personal part. Also, the overall plan, wanted that to be successful--yes. Didn't seem like it was going to be too successful, but I guess it survived two thousand years. Still pretty fragmented, still a lot of work.

M: And distortions left to clear...

Yv: Right.

M: Are some people getting it?

Yv: Are you getting it, Maggie?

M: Sometimes more than others *(laughter)*.

Yv: Yes, you know you're much loved.

M: Thank you.

Yv: Unconditionally, at all times, regardless of thought or act. Thank you for this opportunity to speak. To help.

M: As you understand, it's my deepest honor.

Yv: We love you, too.

M: Is there more for now? Would you like to comment?

Yv: I think all the questions have been answered. Is there anything on that piece of paper you have that needs to be answered now? Because I think we are pretty much done. I mean, we know I lived another sixty years after the ascension and was killed by those full of fear, again it's fear. Fear that their life would be disrupted, fear that maybe they had it wrong. We don't need to review those details here.

M: Do you feel you accomplished what you intended to? Is there anything you would want different?

Yv: Well, I would have liked that the whole world suddenly accepted our Message. And everybody lived in peace and harmony and love forever and ever. (*laughter*) But that didn't happen. I came into that incarnation to help Yeshua. We decided as his brother and companion that would be the most effective. I did that, I played that role as best I could, and I've tried to propagate the Truth, Message of the Truth, whenever I can. So, I have to say that's been success, even though it's not the ideal success that we would all like.

M: I think you've answered this before, but can you answer these to be clear? Did you have a wife or a girlfriend?

Yv: No, there was one or two women I was interested in, but I really dedicated my life to the role with Yeshua.

M: Thank you. And if we can ask you, it's suggested in the Bible, Yeshua was alone without family. Could you please comment on this?

Yv: I think we've been able to demonstrate that we were a family and a community that supported what he did, each with their own interests and skill level, by choice. Many of his siblings were living their own lives, and not active in the ministry. People have taken this as disinterest or non-support, and that's just not true. They loved and supported him with that love, but they had their own lives.

M: I really get the sense from what you've shared the whole community was family.

Yv: Yes.

M: If I could ask, could you let us know, whether you, Yaakov, were counted as one of the apostles?

Yv: No, I was his brother.

M: Were you also called James the Just, or was that someone else?

Yv: Yes, James the Just.

M: Thank you. Are you, Yaakov, also Saint James, buried in Spain?

Yv: No.

M: That's someone else?

Yv: Yes.

M: So, if I may ask, if you were James the Just, then you were not James the Lesser--that was someone else? Is that correct?

Yv: Those were other James's, and you read in the history there were lots of James and Marys and Johns... common names in the community.

M: Thank you so much, is there anything else you would like to share at this time?

Yv: There is no resentment or remorse or anything negative towards any of these folks that played important parts in our lives that ended with harm or death. It just happened. We extend them our love and pray that they will learn to love as well. Unconditionally. Come to the light if they haven't. That's all.

M: Thank you so much. I'd like to express deep gratitude and love to all those beings who shared with us today.

Guest Review
Aaron and Yeshua Provide Further Explanations

November 4, 2017 Saturday, Private Session part one, reviewed by Aaron and Yeshua (Jeshua).

Barbara: This is Barbara, and I'm with Justin. We're looking at his transcript of the latest, the final May 26, 2017 Yaakov transcript. Aaron will incorporate.

{Aaron is reading on through the Yaakov transcript, so this is not a "talk" as such, but responses as he reads. ~~ Justin}

Aaron: I am Aaron. This is information that really needs to come out into the world, because it helps to clarify why Jeshua came, what the issues were around his coming, and who opposed him. I would picture the situation before His coming like a stream feeding from a huge glacier, coming down the mountain and then blocked, dammed, so that the pure water is not coming down into the valley. If you remove one rock, the water starts to flow.

Jeshua did not come to remove all the rocks, because that is the human responsibility, for each human to participate in the removal of the obstacles. He came to help people be more aware that the flow of—I'm using this stream image as a metaphor, of course—the flow of divine Truth is available if they will open their hearts to it. He came to help people remember that the essence of that divine Truth is knowing themselves as divine, as he knew himself as divine. He was not looking for people to put him on a pedestal but to join him up on that pedestal, to be that divinity with Him. This is why so many of you came into the Earth plane, then and now. Some had so completely forgotten that intention, so there's only the tiniest remnant of it buried deep in the human's consciousness. But for many it's now in the accessible consciousness.

This is a short repetition of some of the things in my Earth history transcripts. The archangels—Ariel, Gabriel, Michael, Raphael and the one you call the Dark Angel, Lucifer—I do not know them by these names; they have very different names where I live! These five angels came together pre-Earth with the intention to use their energy to support a highly positively polarized material plane, because, as you say somewhere in the transcript, there have to be the obstacles. You can envision it perfectly on the higher realms, but unless there's something resisting it through which you with your own free will move beyond, then it's blocked. The change doesn't happen.

There was consensus among these five that there could be a material plane with sentient life on it—material sentience, not just light/energy sentience. And that with the heavier vibration of that sentient life on this heavier vibrational planet, they could, through their own free will, bring this light into—I'm finding myself at a loss for words. The basis of their plan is a challenging concept to articulate. One moment...

(pause)

Ariel: I am Ariel. My blessings to you. Aaron refers to me as his teacher, and I was one of the five co-creators of this plan. He's asking me if I will speak about this. There are some early transcripts in your Center in which I speak of the plan, and I would refer you to those. I will be brief.

Ariel cont'd: It is easy to hold that high vibration in a positively polarized, non-material realm. There were, through the universe, various heavier material planes forming, and they were all of a much lower vibration. We saw that negativity established itself within this lower vibration. There was a strong knowing from the five of us that it was possible for there to be a high vibration material plane, and that this so-called Earth plane-to-be could be transformative, almost a seed, for raising heavy density vibration throughout the universe. The seed could be this planet that we would create with our energy and Love. We did not create Earth, as in, "Now there will be a planet;" it came into being in the ways that planets do, took form, took mass through various energy, and so forth. But we held it with light, holding the possibility that the heavy density aspects of it could raise into a very high vibration.

The emphasis was on the life forms, the higher sentient life forms that would live there, and their ability—I'm asking Aaron a bit for help with words; I have the thoughts, he has the words, but I was there and he wasn't, which is why he asked me to speak—that of their own free will choice for the high vibration of love when faced with negative catalyst, with pain, with fear and so forth, that each time they chose Love, they would transform their vibration. Free will to choose Love over fear is the vital ingredient for such transformation, Our intention was to support that into which you as humans are presently moving into the possibility: to know yourselves truly as light and energy, and as high vibration, such a high vibration that nothing negative can remain close. It's not that the high vibration attacks the negativity. It's rather how you would feel if you flew into the sun: at a certain point you'd know it was too hot and turn away because it would burn you up. This high vibration of light is such an anathema to negativity that it will eventually turn away of its own free will. You cannot force it, it must be of its own free will.

Ariel cont'd: You, Justin, spoke in your transcript of the question of Judas. Let us say that Lucifer is another example of the Judas principle. Lucifer has a bad press, as you put it, that he is the devil, the evil one. But there had to be one willing to explore the path of negative polarity so as to prove it is not a viable path. Unfortunately, he became so caught up in his own path and intentions that he lost the reality of Love. He's still trying to make negativity a viable path to liberation. You cannot go into that darkness and end up with light. You cannot go that deep into hatred and end up with Love. He feels that hatred is a viable path, that fear is a viable path. This is not so.

When you reach the end of 6th density negative polarity, it is a dead end. You cannot release self because the negative polarity comes from self. There's nothing to hold the negative polarity together if you release self. And because if you released it at that point, at the high end of 6th density, with negative polarity you would implode, in a sense; the consciousness would be destroyed. There would be no consciousness left to move into 7th and 8th density. Only light, Love, very positive vibration and polarity can move through the end of 6th density into 7th, emerging with intact consciousness. *{see chapter on "Densities" to have a brief summary of densities 1 to 8 and service-to-self versus service-to-others paths. ~~ Justin}*

Ariel: So, the five of us came with the intention to manifest our knowing that a positively polarized heavy density planet was possible with heavy density sentient beings; and that because of Love-based intention, they could move not just their human consciousness, but the whole planet, into a high vibration. This ascension into high vibration is what Jeshua demonstrated. This is what all of you are in the process of doing: releasing what is heavy and negative, finding that which is light and pure and radiant, and transcending into this higher density, while still walking on the Earth.

Life will be much easier then. You won't have to take the hammer and saw and build; you will visualize. Lemuria was a predecessor to the heavy density of the Earth. In Lemuria everything was already 6th density and very high vibration. One could think and create. There was no sense of a separate self so there was no negative thought. One could not do harm because there was no separate self.

Ariel cont'd: Some believed that this is what we were seeking to create, but Lemuria was a glorified dead end. We five who wanted to see what would happen with a heavier density planet said the notion of the separate self is important, because then it is free will that transcends negativity. If you do not have the notion of the separate self then there's nothing to transcend.

So, from Lemuria and through Atlantis, which was the next stage, many beings at that point either left this earth plane or agreed to have the DNA altered so that they would literally forget who they were and why they came. Of course, Lemurians did not thusly agree. They always knew their connection to God, and that they were God, everything was God, and yet that there was this pure radiance from which they were expressing. They totally honored that and could do nothing in violation of that. Once the DNA was altered so there was forgetting, everything shifted. If people got caught up in the small self, they forgot who they were, they forgot divinity.

This was Step One in a progression, a trust in the possibility of the wonder of having a heavy vibrational planet that could raise its vibration with sentient beings that are mass, meat, that can be right there in that divinity rather than separating themselves from it.

So, when the five of us surrounded this mass and supported it as it formed with Love and with light, we lay the groundwork that this planet had the possibility to move from the heavy density mineral, vegetable form into light while retaining the mineral and vegetable forms. We chose to support that, and we continue to support it. The four of us hold the Earth constantly with Love and support every effort to move it into higher vibration.

Aaron, is that sufficient to what you wished me to say? Yes. Aaron will come back. Thank you, my friend. Thank you for the work you are doing.

Aaron: I am Aaron. Thank you, Ariel. So, next step, here. Let us just run through this. I'm not going to comment on very small things.

Aaron cont'd: The triangulation pattern. There was the triangulation pattern in the tomb with these three, and there were also three other caves holding the triangulation at a distance, with several beings in each cave. A lot of the support was done with toning. The caves were distant, but not that far distant. But not right there, not ten feet away; half a mile, a mile. The toning can move through the rock and be enhanced by rock. The toning in this triangular pattern supported what was happening in the tomb. All were trained in this way. So, this is important. You were not there, you were in the tomb. You knew what was going on, but it did not come up in this question. I wanted to make sure that was added.

Also, those who knew what was being attempted, is really broader than Yaakov had stated. Within the Essene community, I'd say half knew and were being trained to participate in some way. Not the little children; the children knew something important was being done, but they only had the gist of it. Those who were above age eleven or so knew and understood more. But about half of the Essene community literally incorporated at that time and into that community because they had some connection previously with Jeshua, and with the intention to support his work in this lifetime. So, he did not just come into some community; he came into a community in which people were waiting with wonder and with Love to welcome him. In which people had been studying for decades, some of them, to know how best to support this transition into a higher consciousness; and understood that he would be the bringer of this higher consciousness and truth.

Justin: As you are talking, I see the Essene community in prayer, holding space during the ascension process.

Aaron: Yes, the whole community was holding that space because most of them who were not the little children understood exactly what was happening. A number of them had prior lifetimes as Lemurians, and some of those were the teachers who understood the whole transformation: what happened during the ascension, and the many skills and practices necessary, which we as a community had learned and practiced to support the ascension. So, it wasn't just prayer, although prayer is vital, but practices like explained in my "Path of Clear Light" book, but far beyond that. These in the book are, if I might state it this way, still beginner practices, but there are much more powerful practices of light and of sound. Many were using these to support the ascension, and before that...

There are so many important complementary practices, and this is what I hope that I can get into further, that the Path of Clear Light is Book One. I see it just as a start. And as people become stable in these practices of light, we can move on to the next step, really what the people in the Essene community were learning. They take you on that path. Because this is what's needed, not just for Jeshua's ascension, but for the ascension of Earth. This is it. Jeshua was demonstrating the ascension for one human. Now each has to do it for the human and for the Earth, and is capable of doing it.

So, there were many who were knowledgeable. When I spoke to Barbara earlier, while she was lying in bed after she read your transcript, she asked me, *Aaron, what part did Nathaniel play in this? What part did Nathaniel's father play? What part did she as Nathaniel's son play?*

{*Aaron was Nathaniel, a shepherd in the time of Yeshua. His father in that life, Isaiah, requested Aaron as Nathaniel to incarnate to assist. Barbara was Mark, Nathaniel's son in that life. ~~ Justin*}

I'd like to talk just a little about this. I was Aaron in a lifetime five hundred years before Jeshua's birth. A beloved spirit to whom I looked as friend and teacher came to me and asked me, would I be willing, having those five hundred years as Aaron, to leave that lifetime and take a new birth to help bring forth all that would come with Jeshua, to help support it? I was very happy to do that.

Aaron cont'd: My father was in that new lifetime named Isaiah. He was a shepherd. He was also a very, I don't know what words to use to describe him, but a highly evolved and awake being, with great knowledge of all of these practices, a teacher. He strongly believed that the learned people in the cities were not open to Jeshua's teaching, to his truth. But the shepherds, the "small people" in the hills, were open. So, he decided that he would not live in the Essene community, although he went back and forth easily. He taught there and was much respected there. But he was a shepherd in the hills to teach the shepherds in simple language. He asked me to come and be his son in that situation and carry on his work. I was to be a shepherd while also trained in the Essene community. So, I also went back and forth.

Hence, I had the ability to talk to everyday people, to put it in simple terms. To know their hardships. And to learn the deep teachings that were being taught in the community and to translate them into terms accessible to those with no education. I was blessed to be a friend of Jeshua. It was not specifically planned that Jeshua and I would be friends. But it was wonderful, we just connected. Of course it's because we had past lives together, and we knew each other instantly. So, we loved each other. We were friends.

At the time of the ascension, the one I was, Nathaniel, was out in the fields with my sheep, and with a great many shepherds who had gathered. This was another strong point of light, that so many of them, having heard of his crucifixion, and who had come to love him, were holding light, not just from the triangulated points but from everywhere. Holding their Love for him. This was also a very powerful support for the ascension.

Justin: I can feel it.

Aaron: So that's just a bit about who I was in that lifetime. And my son, Mark, who Barbara was, was with me that night. He had been training in the Essene community, but because he was only about fourteen at the time of the crucifixion and then the community broke up, he never received the later trainings. His memory is of his anger at Jeshua, what he felt like as betrayal for leaving when he knew he could have chosen to stay.

Aaron cont'd: Mark unfortunately went on to become vocal in non-self-preserving ways. As you pointed out, part of what was needed was if these teachers were to survive, they had to know how to survive. But Mark was an angry teenager and ended up getting himself crucified. He was actually crucified upside-down. They were bored of crucifying people right-side up, so they started crucifying not just Mark but many of them upside-down. So, he did not live long.

Mark got the basics that would sustain him through the coming lifetimes and prepare him for full awakening. I think the strongest basis that he got is his, Barbara's, memories of nights when we had walked with Jeshua and Mark was a young boy, maybe eight, ten years old; just sitting embraced by Jeshua while the men talked around the fire, and feeling the power of Jeshua's energy and love. Those wordless moments took him directly to connection with God, and to beginning to know himself as God. He still needed a number of lifetimes to know what to do with the heavy density human emotions and so forth, the heavy density human body.

As an aside, some of what Barbara is doing right now is working with this heavy density body with things like the wounds, with things like skin cancer surgery and stitches, to release any heavy density energy from this. The whole body is not going to ascend, as it were, in this moment. The body is a human body. But the negative tension and energy that's weighty, cells knocking against themselves, can release. The cells--it's almost a picture of negative and positive polarity. The positive polarity of the cells that love each other and want to come together in intactness, instantly, and the negative polarity of cells that are still traumatized and filled with fear. The cells are learning how trauma can be calmed instantly, bringing instant healing. There's no reason there cannot be instant healing. So, this is part of the evolution into higher polarity for all of you: learning how to work with the physical distortions that come for the human. Greeting them with care and compassion, without giving them any extra strength.

Aaron cont'd: Let me add one thought here. Within that Essene community, one of the things we practiced was instant healing. Children were taught this, also. If a child fell down and scraped his knee, at first with the pain he might cry, and adults would come. They would hold him. And then they would work not just energetically with energy touching the body, but energy coming through them, and drawing from the child's divine energy, and finding that divine energy that exists in every cell; inviting those cells to open themselves, restore themselves; the damaged cells to flush themselves out again with Love. Within a minute or two, the scrape was gone.

The whole community was learning these skills, in part to support the ascension. It was a practical way to teach it. So, it became a skill that was taught even to the youngest children, and this is why the whole community gathered, were able to bring so much energy to Jeshua in the tomb and to support the ascension. Even the young children there could help.

Unless you have questions, let me go further through the transcript.

Aaron: *(reading transcript)* ...Yes, the crystals help... Those in the other caves had very strong crystals that helped support the toning that was happening. They echoed the toning, in a sense.

If there's any place *(reading transcript)* you want me to comment, as I scroll through, please ask. If there's anything specific you want me to speak to, I am happy to do so.

You were all relatively confident. You didn't know that you had been training for this. You came into the incarnation with a plan to do this, and of course, being human, forgot some of that plan. But you had been training for lifetimes to do this. You and Jeshua talked about it on a higher plane before either of you incarnated. You didn't know how it would play itself out, that there would specifically be a crucifixion. You only knew that you were prepared. And Jeshua trusted that you were prepared. So yes, doubt came up, but that was the human side.

Justin: So, should we include that concept in this, that Jeshua and I discussed this previously, and the human mind didn't remember?

Aaron: Yes, but it was not just Jeshua and you; it was Jeshua and all of you. (**Justin**: Right.) That's why all of this Essene community came together. They were specifically volunteers, and trained through a number of lifetimes and many discussions with Jeshua to come together to do this. And those that took birth as children, the new humans, were old souls that had agreed to participate. Nothing was chance.

"...these were some of the techniques... that you thought you were being trained in those ways for information to be used later, if you wanted to." Not specifically, Justin. You knew that something was going to happen with Jeshua, that there was going to be some form of raising of light and energy. You had no idea how it would play itself out. When he was taken from the garden and you realized, yes, now is the time, you still didn't know he was going to be crucified, only this is the time that we have been training for, for lifetimes. This is our opportunity to support the ascension of Jeshua and the whole world. So, you knew that. And I think your doubt, when you talk about it there, when Yaakov talks about it there, was more a bit of the human coming through.

Part of the training was what we do with the Vipassana. Seeing thoughts arise and not becoming self-identified with those thoughts. Some of you were more deeply trained in that than others. You were still human, and you did not yet have the high vibration and training to enable you to watch a thought arise and not get caught up in it even a little bit. So here, a little bit of lack of confidence. Human! Not bad, just human.

...Yes, Yaakov was in and out of the last supper...

...Yes, "...he wanted them to remember him daily..."— not him but the Truth. And it's this heavy density bread that grows from the Earth and the wine that comes from the fruit of the grapes, that this also is ascending into this high vibration. Eventually, when this vibration is so high, you as humans will need to eat very little. Just the air you breathe will nourish you. But there will be joy in eating, and the Earth will want to offer you the food. Because you are human, the taste is a joyful taste. But you will not so much eat to fill the belly as eat to thank the Earth for what it gives.

Aaron cont'd: I'm scrolling through, now... I'm onto page 58 now... The controversy about Judas— yes... Judas knew and did not know what he was doing. He obeyed. He did not do it in any sense for greed. He did it because it was what he was asked to do, but he also knew that he was setting something in motion that was going to be terribly painful. He didn't know how it would play out, but he knew it would play out in a very painful way. He loved Jeshua enough to do what he was asked.

Now we come to Jeshua on page 62 of the transcript. All clear, all very clear... The ascension needed to be completed... Now I would take this a bit further. One moment, Jeshua says he'd like to take it further, since it's his story...

Jeshua: I loved you then and I love you now.

I am Jeshua, and we're reading on page 62. At first, I had less ability— when I say, "at first," immediately. The ascension was basically the change on a cellular level, so that each cell would be at such a high vibration that any heaviness was gone from it. But I needed to retain enough of the cellular structure not to simply dissolve. Consciousness would not go anywhere, but I wanted to maintain some level of the body.

In the Buddhist tradition they talk about the "rainbow body." Have you heard of this? Well, I have seen this. When I was Jeshua I saw it numerous times among the great Masters. After the body dies, usually with the Master sitting in a lotus position, consciousness leaves the body. The body remains sitting. They offer some incense and say some prayers and then close up the building. People chant and pray around the building for about a week. Throughout that week, rainbow lights emit from the building. There's a constant display of rainbow light 24/7. When the rainbow light—I'm asking Aaron—he is laughing at my example! It's like popcorn: you listen, and when it stops popping, you know it's done. When the rainbow light ceases, they open the door, and there's nothing left but the hair and nails. Everything else has completely dissolved because there were no impurities, no karma in any of the cells. The body simply dissolved.

Jeshua cont'd: I did not do that because I did not die in my training period. I was taught *how* it was done, but the challenge for me was that I could not fully dissolve, since I was not to die in the usual sense. That would have been easier. I had to retain some energy of the cellular material so I could become visible. And in fact, I *was* visible.

So yes, immediately I was not solid. But very quickly I became solid enough that people could really see me. I did not stay in that area and talk with you, with the disciples as much, as it was time to go. And I went, with Mary. She had studied techniques, and was not yet perfected but advanced in techniques to ascend without dying the body, to ascend the body into a less heavy cellular structure. And I helped her in that, to learn it and do it.

The two of us moved to the area of Europe where we lived, and then elsewhere through the world. We had children. We lived as humans do but without any heavy human emotion. But I did not die. There were various brother/sisterhoods there similar to the Essene brotherhood where the crucifixion took place, brotherhoods in that part of Europe and in some of the places where you had traveled a year or two ago, that supported what we were doing, and also worked to continue this process of ascension of the Earth. They were not the Essene community but a different name, but they were all supporting the same direction of the work.

If no questions, I'll go on.

Justin: Do you want me to explain this about Mary and you?

Jeshua: I think it would be fine to take this transcript and simply run it side by side so that you don't have to try to insert it. Rather, just to say at the beginning, "Aaron and Jeshua speak some expansion or some explanation of what I have experienced here that may enrich the topic for you."

"Other things to do to take the message of truth forward..." The disciples did the best they could, and I love them very much. But they were not fully awakened beings, and they did not know fully what they were doing. So, they did what the human mind told them to do, and thus they created a church, which is not what I would have done.

Jeshua: Let me look through this a bit...

(Jeshua starts a new recording file).

Justin: I am glad Aaron knows how to use that because I don't! (referring to Barbara's iPad).

Jeshua: He has watched Barbara so many times. I've watched in the background but not paid precise attention.

All of this is accurate. It would take us hours to go through it... The explanation of the Lord's Prayer, yes... Now, reading what Peter said. I repeat: I have much Love for Peter. As he said, he did the best he could, and I agree. Now let me add something here.

Peter said he did the best he could, and yes, there were distortions. These disciples were not enlightened beings. I knew as they were my disciples and I was teaching them, that there had to be distortions. It was part of what—how can I best phrase this? If it had come out perfect without distortions, it would have been on a level up here, and the people with the lower vibration could not have even realized there was a message. They would have said, "What? He arose from the dead? That's crazy." They wouldn't have taken it to heart in any way. There had to be somebody that could transmit it from that vibration down to here. These disciples had to be a means of transfer from a higher to a lower vibration. And to do that it was really necessary that they would bring in some distortions. Doing the best they could, but still making it accessible to the human <u>because</u> there were distortions. Because the humans were not yet ready to hear it on the highest vibration.

Now you are ready. I certainly am not advocating the decease of the church, but I think it will become increasingly unimportant in people's lives, or understood in a different way.

Justin: Can't the church evolve?

Jeshua: Perhaps. It will have to let go of a lot. It's the question, if you have an old house that is falling apart, is it easier to tear it down and build new, or is it easier to try to renovate it? I think both will happen, so that there will be many of the young people of today who do not practice religion but spirituality, and are not interested in churches or structure of that sort at all. They will lead the way. But then my hope would be that the church, seeing what is happening, and that some of these young people will move into more formal religious structures—when I say the church, not just Christian church but all the formal religions—that the church will begin to see their purpose in a new way; that religion is a path to knowing the Divine, and that's all it is. And to living that knowing of the Divine. Then the church will have an important role to play, free of dogma and ideas of ultimate good and evil, or of heaven and hell.

"Some that listened wanted to understand, and they did understand some." There are others who didn't believe at all...

"...to do the work without getting killed..." —you did that.

"... to serve those populations separately..." —yes. Some of those in the Jewish hierarchy did not want my teachings perpetuated. Some of those in the Gentile population also did not want it perpetuated. I think it's important to add that. You saw it from your background as the Essene, but the Gentiles were just as much against many of my teachings. This concerns us because in the world there is still so much the idea the Jews killed Jesus. It's important that people understand that everyone, various traditions, were frightened by what I taught. Frightened because of course they were centered in their egos, and what I taught was asking them to release the ego. And that terrified them, whatever religion they came from. It took away their personal power and sense of control.

So somewhere in here you say the Jews killed James, and I think it's important that you correct that, if it feels appropriate to you. "Jews and others." More accurately, Fear killed me. Hate based in fear killed me, or attempted to do so. Here you were speaking as Yaakov from his understanding of it at that point. That's the only place where I wish you would slightly alter your transcript.

"Love, always choose Love..." I thank my friend Aaron for bringing that message so clearly to the Earth at this time, and Barbara also. Always choose Love.

Aaron, may I see— I have not seen— you've spoken of the end of your book *(The Path of Clear Light, published by Deep Spring Press, January 2018).* May I see it? Yes. Where do I see it? ...

(reading, with comments)
So, please practice!
Watch the movements
from darkness to light,
from fear to love,
from contraction to spaciousness — without trying to fix anything.
Simply observe the old habits.
Then find the courage to say a gentle but firm "no" to the unwholesome habits
that would keep you small,
limited,
and in darkness.
Each time you consciously choose Love and light, you release eons of old, harmful, habitual reaction and karma.

Jeshua: That's what we were just talking about. That's why you have to be on the earth plane to do it.

With such ongoing daily practice, know your power to CHOOSE Light. This is not earthly light, as a metaphor, but Light, the eternal and unchanging. Enter its direct experience.
Glow!!!
Jeshua: I like that!
Whether it is an actual glow,
or as metaphor for the radiance felt in the heart. You know how it looks when you see another being glowing with joy and light.
Just do the same.
Glow!!!
Yet again, I say, you do have a choice.

But if at times you cannot choose Light, if it is too frightening,
too bright,
be gentle with yourself
and choose kindness to the self while you rest
and ready the self to try again.
Be like the climber attempting a towering peak. The climber
must look up and know the destination, but also look down to find
firm footing.
Hold to both,
the Light in all its perfection and radiance, and the mud
underfoot.
But when you pause,
look up,
rest for a bit,
know where you are going,
and remember your intention
to ascend that peak which is your true home.

Jeshua*:* I like the way, Aaron, that you use the word "ascend."

While you rest,
allow yourself to meditate
and to re-experience Light,
even if it feels distant and unreachable.
Soon, that Light can become as familiar as the air you breathe.
Here is the gradual growth of Awareness mingled with Clear
Light. Spaciousness is the doorway.
Practice until Light is with you always: sometimes in the
foreground, sometimes in the background.
Practice until you can never again lose that Light.
I will walk the path with you,
just out of sight beyond the turn of the road.
Walk with my love, Aaron
Jeshua: Thank you, Aaron. This is the ascension.

Reading this paragraph from page 70 of Justin's transcript...
"Jeshua so loved the world, he came and he was the messenger. He
knew it would be difficult..." This is clear. Thank you for getting
that so clearly from me. *(smiling)* The message got distorted.

"...to practice it. To REALLY learn it. You're being challenged to learn those new skills of unconditional Love and of working through the fear, the anger, the sadness, whatever that emotion is that you experience here. If you don't learn to work through those, and arrive at Love, you haven't learned it... You have to get the lesson in order to learn it."

I really have no additional comments on what you've said here. You speak very clearly. You have channeled me clearly. I appreciate that. It is of course incomplete, but all channeling is incomplete. We could talk through you for days. "Are some people getting it? Are you getting it?" Yes, you're getting it.

Here is the place I meant. "...we know I was killed by the Jewish leaders, again it's fear." I was killed by fear. I would take out the word "Jewish"; I was killed by fear. Page 74... "We know I was killed by fear." Period. Just that.

People were so afraid. It's the fear—can you imagine how you might feel as a human if suddenly beings came in a spaceship and, a plant was bent, a tree was bent, and they were just able to reach up and straighten it? And they were able to snap their fingers and a beautiful crystal structure arose? And they used no speech to communicate, just looked in each other's eyes? You would feel overwhelmed. You would feel small, unsafe.

People were terrified by my ascension. They were terrified by the ideas that were being presented, that there was something beyond this everyday life, something which the Jews did not teach and the Gentiles did not really believe. None of them believed really in an afterlife, at that point. Buddhism got it a bit closer, without a belief in an afterlife, but with the idea of karma and reincarnation. Hinduism fell short because of the deeply held ideas of karma as punishment. There's no heaven or hell but one moves into more heavenly realms as one evolves. Heavenly because you're not caught up with fear and hatred. Or one moves into a hell realm filled with negativity. It's up to you which you choose. You can do it 10,000 times until you get it right, if necessary. Eventually you'll get it right.

(typing) Aaron is asking me to do this. Is this correct, Aaron? He says, almost... He says he will send this to you... (Justin: Good.)

I think this is it unless you have other questions for me.

Justin: The entity identified itself as the Knowing. What or who is that?

Jeshua: The speaker identified itself as the Knowing... Let me look so I can see exactly what you're talking about... All right. So here you've used a term I would not have used, but it's a very useful term.

I am no longer Jeshua; this is not really Jeshua speaking to you. If we use the term 'Jeshua,' we think of the bit of light, intelligence and Love that took birth in that human plane and became the human, Jeshua. So, he is contained, his knowing is contained, in what Jeshua knew. But I am so far evolved beyond Jeshua that when you call me now, this is Jeshua speaking to you and also what you call here, and what is understood here as the Knowing. I would call it the Christ or awakened one. Probably best not to use in this transcript, because the word 'Christ' is often misinterpreted. I could use the word 'Buddha' as the one who is awake, but that term creates confusion with my brother Siddhartha Gautama and others that are thusly awakened.

Jeshua was the human expression. The Christ is the whole, the Christ consciousness that I am. We could call it the I Am. That could be a good term to use. The "I Am" is speaking, because the term 'the Christ' will be misunderstood and create separation. You are all the Christ. You are all the ones who are awakening.

Justin: Is this also what is meant by the Holy Spirit?

Jeshua: Yes, that's another term that you could use.

(taping unexpectedly quit, starting a new audio file)

Aaron: We lost some of part two, the last part, five, ten minutes...

Citta is the Pali word for consciousness. There is mind consciousness and body consciousness. Mind touches an object and thought arises, thinking consciousness, as remembering, planning. Body touches an object, resultant in body sense consciousness. Pressure, heat. Seeing consciousness; hearing consciousness, tasting or smelling consciousness. Every consciousness, or citta, takes an object. With mundane consciousness, these are all mundane objects.

Awakened consciousness, Christ consciousness, or whatever you wish to call it, can touch supramundane objects. The Holy Spirit no longer experiences mundane consciousness in the same way. It can perceive, but it doesn't perceive solid wood, for example. It perceives all the cells and molecules that create the wood. It perceives the tree there; it perceives something alive, not just a wood desk. This level of consciousness perceives unity and Creation, and also destruction. But nothing ever is destroyed, it simply tumbles under and comes out again, expressing constantly.

I'm not sure if I've fully answered your question. I think there's something there that I'm missing.

Justin: Is the Holy Spirit a consciousness of God, the Source?

Aaron: I would not say it that way, Justin. You're asking is the Holy Spirit a consciousness of God?

Justin: A manifest consciousness of God?

Aaron: So, is it God's eyes, ears, heart, in a sense? The perceiving aspect of God and the outward expression of God? The voice of God? Give me a minute. I understand your question; I want to think of the best way to explain what I understand as the Holy Spirit...

Yes, we would say that Jeshua is not only Holy Spirit. He was the Son, now he is Holy Spirit. But the Trinity is One. There is no separation in it. Consciousness, what we call Father/Mother/Creator/Divinity, it is omni-conscious. It does not need any extension of itself to be conscious. It simply is, and in its true being it is conscious. It is conscious of objects. Every consciousness takes an object. Everything is its object, but it does not see it as the human does; it sees it in its unity as well as its diversity. It sees separation simply as the way the fingers look separate, but knowing they're all part of the hand. *(Aaron is holding his hand behind a sheet of paper so only the fingers show above the top. ~~ Justin)*

Aaron cont'd: Jeshua now is not so much knower of God, or consciousness, or expression. Jeshua is—are you familiar with the three kayas? Dharma kaya, let's call it God; nirmanakaya, the material world; sambhogakaya, the bridge. Jeshua at present is more the bridge. God does not need that bridge to connect; humans need that bridge to connect. When you move into what we might term Christ or awakened consciousness, then that consciousness becomes the bridge that allows us to move into the direct experience of the Divine, and thusly know ourselves as part of that Divine, and not as separate.

Can you read this? *(asking Justin to read a page, tape paused)* I have just had Justin read page 65 of "Path of Clear Light," about the three kayas. So, God is everything. It does not need any expression of itself to know everything because it IS everything, just as you don't need anything to let you know there's an itch on your little toe. There's constant connection. But from the nirmanakaya level, the human level, lower consciousness level, we need something to help us move up into and connect with the higher consciousness. At first it may be just kindness, a smile. This can pull us out of the low-density human vibration into a slightly higher vibration. But as we become ready, then we can turn to one such as Jeshua, who is holding his hand out and offering to help lift us up, to ascend into the higher consciousness as he did. So, he is the bridge.

Does that answer your question?

Justin: I am going to contemplate it.

Aaron: We can Skype with this, we can talk further as is necessary. The whole question of the Trinity and three kayas is addressed very nicely in a book I believe with Thich Nhat Hanh and a Zen master. Barbara can show you the book. It's one of the topics that they discuss with some level of sophistication. I do not say they are identical, the three kayas and the Trinity, but there's a wonderful congruency to them. I would be happy, not now but I would be happy at another time to talk further about it.

Unless you have further questions from me, let us close now, knowing we can talk.

There were times, you as Yaakov saying, there would be times when it would just be easier if Jeshua was there to speak instead of me. You must have missed him so much, yes.

Now, he could make himself visible, but he also knew that he had to not make himself visible to those who would use that as a way of carrying their fear and belief in limitations further. He did make himself more visible to some than to others.

Karma

Yaakov and Justin

During the regression, Maggie could astutely feel the deep pain and frustration Yaakov was feeling during the last session. After the session, she felt it important to bring the sense of these feelings to my (Justin's) attention and inquire how I felt about it (she was being a most excellent therapist). At first, I was simply reiterating the justification that Yaakov presented: they were all a part of the community and all needed to help and know their roles. A justification that pushed feelings aside.

Later, while remembering the scenes and Yaakov's feelings, I became able to manifest and discuss those feelings in a way Yaakov was not allowed. It did take a few days to process those feelings. One afternoon, tears began streaming down my face as I finally fully felt, acknowledged, and gave credence to long-suppressed feelings of immense grief. Grief Yaakov had for losing his brother, for knowing he was tortured and crucified, tending gently to the wracked body in the tomb. Resentment for not being allowed to grieve at the time, instead his feelings brushed aside for the importance of the duties at hand--always the duties that were more important than self. Frustration that came with accepting the leadership role after Yeshua left, but wasn't really gone. The grief of losing Yeshua to other pursuits, as he, Yaakov, stayed as agreed. The grief of losing his family as they fled for safety to France and England, and he stayed in Jerusalem, alone.

I know intellectually that on the other side of the veil, these human emotions were not there. I know I had the camaraderie of my dear friend, Yeshua, without angst. Yet, on this plane there are these strong emotions to deal with. Prior to this project, in this incarnation, I respected Yeshua as a messenger and prophet, but saw and felt him as a distant historical figure with whom I could interact in the spirit realm through prayer/meditation. We had a working relationship for questions. He always seemed a bit friendlier than I knew what to make of, but attributed that to his unconditional love for everyone. I had a wall up between us. A wall of separation. Now that wall has melted. It came tumbling down with the tears shed, emotions acknowledged and healed. Now, we can interact like brothers and friends with an ease I am sure we have on the other side of the veil. It is such a relief!

How does this feel in this human body now? There is a calmness and a healing. Those old feelings have all been replaced with love and compassion for all of us, all our roles. The bond of brotherhood and friend has been restored without the niggling wedge of grief, frustration and resentment.

I realize as Justin how I have carried that sense of duty forward as well. I am very busy with a sense of service, sometimes to the exclusion of my personal life. Definitely, I have pushed potential partners to the side, feeling that it is not fair to someone else to pursue my life of service and not be a good partner to them. Spending time with family or friends is always a juggle and feels more like setting an appointment; in fact, if I don't schedule it, it often gets forgotten. I am working on a better balance this time.

I needed to ask why there was this unresolved human emotion here in this incarnation, when I knew better on the other side. Here is that discussion:

Justin: So, the frustration and mild resentment that Yaakov had with Jeshua leaving but not gone, there was some residual in this incarnated body. And now it appears healed.

Jeshua: You loved me very much. You felt frustration that you could not follow me. I think you would have been crucified with me, if allowed. You did not have the training for the ascension. You knew that I had to do my work. You did not want to let me go. You were angry with me for leaving you. You were angry because you could not come where I was going, because you did not know the techniques to raise the body in that way. But I loved you then and I love you now, and there is nothing to forgive. And I hope there is nothing for which I must ask your forgiveness, but if there is, please forgive me...

You have your own path to supporting the ascension of the Earth. You come from a wider background than I did. In other words, have lived on so many different planes, more than I have. And your work is not just the ascension of the Earth but the ascension of the universe, a far larger task. And you are doing very well with your work. So, trust yourself. The Earth leads the way, but the universe must then be prepared to follow.

Justin: So, my question. On the other side of the veil, I know this, but the human emotions incarnate with the body.

Jeshua: *(laughing)* This is why I love vipassana! Please practice. Practice until you come to the place where emotion comes up, there's able to be immense compassion for the human experiencing that emotion, and also nothing sticky to which the emotion can adhere, creating karma, but it's simply known as arisen from conditions and passing away.

Aaron is my comrade here. I depend on Aaron to teach this. It's so important.

Justin: So, *(for me)* the human component of the spirit continued to incarnate with this emotion until now.

Jeshua: The human will continue to incarnate with emotion, with any given emotion or any specific habit, until that karma is purified. Love and forgiveness purify it. Then there's nothing left to which it can adhere. Gradually the human knows that nothing ever happened, it was just the flow of conditions. Immense compassion is held around the humans experiencing this flow of conditions. But finally, consciousness opens up to broad awareness. Aaron can speak about these things. I understand them; he has the vocabulary for them. But there is no longer a sense of a belief of a separate self that experienced it. And yet there is compassion for that illusory self that did experience it. That compassion releases it fully.

Justin: I find it interesting that for 2,000 years this stuck to the human component.

Jeshua: That's a relatively short time for it to stick, Justin. (Me: Okay!) Remember, you were not incarnate all of that 2,000 years, and for at least 1,000 of those years you were on other planes and somewhat beyond the veil, and knowing deeply who you were and what you were doing and were being trained. So then, when it was time to come back to the Earth plane, obviously this karma tagged along.

Justin: Interesting...

Jeshua: There was certainly an intention for the human, not a conscious intention but an intention to meet Aaron in this lifetime, and Barbara too, perhaps, but more specifically Aaron, and connect with him to help you release. And he did not need to do much to help you learn how to release, only to remind you: let it go! Then you knew how to do it. You are doing it; still in process!

Justin: Aaron has been instrumental in helping me to remember.

As Aaron and I teach, acknowledge these human emotions, which are each challenges and teachers in their own right. Acknowledge, learn from them, and transmute them to Love and compassion and forgiveness. Aaron does a wonderful job of teaching this process in his book, "Presence, Kindness and Freedom" and the newly released book, "Path to Clear Light." I highly recommend them as work books to help one learn to work through emotions in a healthy spiritual manner. ~~ Justin

DENSITIES

This section will briefly explain the concept of densities referred to in Archangel Ariel's, Yeshua's, and Aaron's information. A more thorough discussion can be obtained from LLresearch.org website, "The Law of One" channelings and discussions.

There are 8 densities:

1 Elements: fire, water, air, mineral   (body)
2 plants and animals   (body/mind)
3 humans   (body/mind/spirit)
4 beings working on love and knowledge
5 beings working on wisdom
6 another level of beings working on unity of wisdom and love balance
7 Angelic and Light Being realm who were created as is and did not evolve through the densities; and those who have evolved and now are in 7th prior to joining "the all" in 8th
8 The All, the original creative Source, no separation of self

1st density, these elements have a consciousness and an existence but are not self-aware like the other levels. These are said to have a "body" complex, it is comprised of the molecular elements.

2nd density, it is more difficult to understand the difference between 2nd and 3rd density in the animal realm. Both plants and animals have consciousness and some self-awareness. Many people argue that they have "spirits," but the term spirit in 3rd density is different from the "mind/body complex" being of 2nd density. 2nd density beings have a different level of consciousness. They do not create or problem solve or plan in the same manner as 3rd, they do not ask "why?" Groups of animals use their local resources and limit their living group size dependent upon these resources by instinct. They move on or break up if their size becomes too large for their resources. Humans can create (to an extent) more resources to support a larger group size: build aqueducts, animal husbandry, agriculture, build structures. 3rd density understands seasons and time. Animals and plants understand there is dark-light/night-day, but they do not understand why, or even ask why. They do not contemplate building a vehicle to get to the moon or see the stars as other potential life sources. They don't think much about other species or the interdependency of species. But they are evolving more on Earth to have more compassion. Hence, we see some members of some species caring for others: a cat nursing a squirrel, a lioness protecting a baby gazelle instead of eating it. 2nd density accepts a Creator but does not create a story or dogma about it. 2nd is mostly in the present without plans for future. 2nd density can evolve to 3rd. This typically occurs with trees and pets.

3ʳᵈ density, the goal of 3ʳᵈ density with a "body/mind/spirit" complex is to learn about Love and compassion and to understand we are not separate from Creator. There is a veil of forgetting between the 3ʳᵈ density incarnated being and Creative Source and the other densities. This veil creates an illusion of separateness. One must make an effort to remember/learn that one is not separate, that we all are a part of the vast Creation. As Aaron explains: each is as a drop of water that can appear separate, yet be a part of the ocean. In this 3ʳᵈ density with a sense of separateness, some beings make decisions for only themselves, they see themselves separate from all creation and their needs above all others.' These beings are on a "service to self" path, which is often termed "negative polarity." Other beings acknowledge each is a part of the whole and others are important as well. When these beings make decisions taking others' well-being into account as well as their own, they are on a "service to others" path, which is termed "positive polarity."

4ᵗʰ density and beyond

Density refers to the amount of light vibration a being has. The more light one has, the higher the vibration, and less solid the being appears. In 4ᵗʰ density and above, most of these beings are not visible to 3ʳᵈ density beings due to the different vibration and intensity of light.

Before beings can move onto 4ᵗʰ density, they each need to make a choice to be positive/service to others, or negative/service to self. Beings continue to incarnate in 3ʳᵈ density form and existence until they are consistent with that choice. If greater than 50% of one's decisions are service to others, then a positive polarity has been chosen and this individual spirit will go on to 4ᵗʰ density positive. If 90% of decisions are service to self, then that spirit goes onto 4ᵗʰ density negative.

The pathways are separate in 4th, 5th and early 6th density. The positive polarity beings coalesce into social complexes starting in 4th density. Beings can still identify as separate, but they are all interrelated thought-wise. Because they are positively polarized, there is Love, compassion and support for each other as difficult times arise and lessons need to be learned. The negative polarized beings develop hierarchies, each jockeying for their place, using fear and manipulation to maintain and optimally advance their standings. They each want to be more important than the other, love of self is all, for others do not count except to be used.

In late **6th density**, the spirit must make a decision. It cannot remain *negatively polarized/ put oneself first* and still become a part of the whole. It either stays in early 6th density or accepts a positive polarity concept of Love and the importance of others and changes paths.

At this point in the explanations about densities, lots of questions usually arise which is beyond the scope of this book. I invite you to read discussions on these concepts in the "Law of One" and on the LL research website. Questions that arise about the nuances of the densities are well reviewed here.

For our purposes, the summary provided here should help to understand the information provided in this book.

When Yeshua says, *"There's no heaven or hell but one moves into more heavenly realms as one evolves. Heavenly because you're not caught up with fear and hatred. Or one moves into a hell realm filled with negativity. It's up to you which you choose. You can do it 10,000 times until you get it right, if necessary. Eventually you'll get it right."*

.... he is saying you have as many times as you need to incarnate, be challenged, learn your lessons until you understand and make the choices that allow you to move on. Manifest in this process is the Universal Law of Free Will. We each have the right of free will with every decision we make. We can partner with God/Creator/Yeshua/our higher self and other guides for advice, but optimally our choices are up to each of us, every step of the way. Each choice is a new opportunity.

And when Archangel Ariel is discussing Lucifer's being stuck on a path of hatred and he cannot evolve further without imploding, he is talking about the need to shift from early 6th density negative to 6th density positive.

CONTROVERSIES

Historically, there are many controversies. I asked about a few of the most common ones and here is what I was told.

What was the reason behind John the Baptist baptizing Jesus?

Recall the scene:

John is at the river baptizing people. Understand that sacred bathing is a required ritual for Jewish people before entering the temple and in order to enter the baths for the temple in Jerusalem, one had to pay money. There were many who therefore could not pay for the ritual bath and could not enter the temple and they were considered "unclean." John was baptizing people free of charge. What right did this man have to do this? If you were baptized by John, were you cleansed of your sins?

Why did Jesus allow John to baptize him? Did he need to be baptized by John? Jesus could enter the temple baths, why did he go to John?

Jesus was pointing out that in many ways some of the religious rituals had become just that, rituals. And these rituals were often beyond the average person such they could no longer participate in sacred rituals that should be for all, not reserved for the wealthy or privileged.

God blessed John and Jesus with a sign of the dove. He gave a public blessing and legitimization to John the Baptist as he baptized all who came (without payment) for cleansing in the river. He gave a public blessing and legitimization to Jesus who was doing the work of God, our Father, the Abba. A sign was given that "these men are doing my work. Listen to them." John and Jesus would have done the work regardless, but here was a public statement, endorsement and blessing from God.

Did James the Just write the "James Epistle?"
James the Just did not actually write the James Epistle. Someone else wrote it and essentially gave him credit for two reasons.

Much, but not all, of what is in the Epistle is what James the Just had spoken, so the writer was attributing the topics to its original source.

The writer wanted it to carry the weight of the authority of James the Just.

What did Jesus mean when he was quoted as saying:
Luke 14:25-27 Easy-to-Read Version (ERV)
²⁵ Many people were traveling with Jesus. He said to them, ²⁶ "If you come to me but will not leave your family, you cannot be my follower. You must love me more than your father, mother, wife, children, brothers, and sisters—even more than your own life! ²⁷ Whoever will not carry the cross that is given to them when they follow me cannot be my follower.

Yeshua explains this has been quoted a bit out of context. He was speaking specifically to those interested in following him physically as he journeyed from village to village. He was not speaking about following his spiritual message.

He was not advocating for people to follow him physically on the road. He was explaining: you will be gone for days, weeks, months. What will happen to your families? Will you leave your wife, your children, your parents, your job, your crops? He was warning about the dangers on the road from bandits and irate people--will you risk your life? Unless you are willing to give all this up and risk all these things, do not come with me. He did not want men to abandon their families, he was not encouraging people to leave everything behind to follow him on the road. He wanted people to think very carefully about such a choice.

There is a spiritual component if one chooses to follow his teachings, they may lose family and friends if these people turn away due to the new beliefs. But one may stay with family and friends, even if they are non-believers. He was not instructing those who choose to follow him spiritually to leave their families.

John: 14:6

No one comes to the Father except through me

Jeshua: John was trying to raise my divinity to those he spoke. What I said was, "No one comes to the Father except through these ways." To choose Love, every time, choose Love, compassion, forgiveness...that is the way to our Father, this is the way to each of our own divinity. I am not the only one who has taught this. Many before and many after teach this. This is the way, I am but one teacher, one messenger. I am not a gatekeeper. I am a bridge, a way, a path to the Source of Unconditional Love and Light.

Mathew 27.46, Psalms 22: 1

My God, My God, why have you forsaken me?

Imagine you are hanging on a cross, your weight on your palms and feet spiked with nails, you can barely breathe, yet you try to talk...those nearby did not hear all that I said, "My God! Father, thank you for not forsaking me." What was heard was, "My God ...forsaking me...." This in turn, was extrapolated to be, "My God, My God, why have you forsaken me?" often presuming it related back to Psalm 22:1.

Who was the Beloved Disciple?

John 20:2 NIV

So she came running to Simon Peter and the other disciple, the one Jesus loved, and said, "They have taken the Lord out of the tomb, and we don't know where they have put him!"

Mary Magdalene came running to James and Peter, who were discussing what to do next now that Jesus had "died." James and Peter were the new leaders after the ascension, they had much to discuss. James was the "disciple Jesus loved" or "beloved disciple," but not named. Consistent with the rest of the Bible, James the brother of Jesus, is rarely acknowledged in the Bible despite he is almost always in attendance. Confusion persists when James is referred to as a disciple, yet he was not actually a disciple because he was the brother and companion of Jesus, and subsequently the leader of the Judean followers of Jesus. Given James was usually in attendance to his brother, some often put him in the category of disciple.

Cast of Speakers and Helpers

Name	Abbreviations used in transcript	Comments
Archangel Ariel Archangel Gabriel		Arch angels are 7th density beings
Aaron		Discarnate 6th density being channeled by Barbara Brodsky
Yeshua	Ya	Jesus of Nazareth, the Christ, Jeshua
Yaakov	Yv	James the Just, brother of Jesus/Yeshua
Mary	Ma	Mary Magdalene, assistant and beloved to Yeshua
Joseph of Arimathea	JA	Wealthy tin merchant, uncle to Yeshua and Yaakov
Peter	P	Apostle to Yeshua, founder of subsequent Catholic Church
Justin		Present day human, was once Yaakov
Maggie	M	Therapist leading hypnosis induction and questions

Brief Genealogy

"Grandmother" is Anna: mother to Mary and Joseph of Arimathea

Mary: mother to Yeshua and Yaakov. She is referenced but does not speak in this transcript.

Mary Magdalene, Beloved to Yeshua, sister to Martha (recall Lazarus their brother who arose from death, in the Bible)

Acknowledgements

As mentioned in the introduction, this two-person project became much bigger than ever expected.

Sincere thanks are extended to everyone involved to bring this work forward, then and now.

First, and foremost, as I explained in the introduction, this work could not have been started, let alone completed, without the expertise, love, compassion and friendship of Maggie. Thank you for agreeing to take this journey with me, to lie down your fears, and trust in the vision and the help given. We could not have done this without you. The gifts, experience, intuition and professionalism you brought to this project is of the highest quality. I am humbly grateful for all your assistance, and to your spouse who was patient and kind while I invaded your home and monopolized your time.

It has been an honor to work with our spirit helpers, we thank you for your eternal love and compassion that support and guide us in this challenging vibration of incarnation.

Archangels Ariel and Gabriel; Yeshua; Aaron; Mary
All our helpers, be they unnamed

And our other guest speakers and the roles they played then and now, thank you for your dedicated work and giving us your voice here:
Joseph of Arimathea, Peter.

To Barbara Brodsky, my friend and a teacher. I honor the brave and strong woman you are. Thank you for all you do for this world.

Accolades to Heidi Walter who edited this book, she is an invaluable gem. Heidi, thank you for your expertise and attention to detail. Thank you for the ease of your assistance. It truly has been a pleasure to work with you cleaning up my typos, incorrect verb tenses, and all the other help needed to polish up this book for readers.

The old friends and new friends who have been proofing this work, your comments and excitement for this work are gratefully accepted.

The Deep Spring board and community members for your work and support as we progress in enlightenment.

Janice Keller for many, many long hours of typing transcriptions for years to bring the Deep Spring members' work forward to the world, and those who assist her in this consuming work. Thank you for that work. But at this time, I also want to thank you for transcribing the "Review" section for this book so that I did not have to transcribe or type it myself!

I am always thankful for the unconditional love my family and friends share with me. They don't always understand what I am doing, but they love and support me regardless, even in my long silences. I don't know that I would do as well as I do without it. Mom, thanks for not thinking I am crazy; and for making me take that typing class in high school.

With love and compassion, Bless us all.

RECOMMENDED READING

Aaron, expressed through Barbara Brodsky 2017, *The Path of Clear Light*, Deep Spring Press, Ann Arbor, MI.

Aaron expressed through Barbara Brodsky, 2003, *Presence, Kindness and Freedom*, Deep Spring Press, Ann Arbor, MI.

Carla Rueckert, Don Elkins, James McCarty, 1981, Ra, *The Law of One*, www.llresearch.org

Clair Heartsong, 2002, *Anna, Grandmother of Jesus*, Spiritual Educational Endeavors publishing, USA.

Clair Heartsong, 2010, *Anna, the Voice of the Magdalenes*, Spiritual Educational Endeavors Publishing, USA.

Marvin W Meyer, *The Naj Hammadi Scriptures*, 2007. E-book published 2013.

Rex Weyler, 2008, **The Jesus Sayings**, House of Anansi Press, Toronto, ON

www.Deepspring.org archives

www.thenazareneway.com/james_the_brother_of_jesus.htm

About the Author

Justin James is a member of Deep Spring sangha out of Ann Arbor, MI. He is a parent, grandparent, teacher, and lover of life and learning.

Made in the USA
Lexington, KY
22 November 2019